GPS
Afloat

GPS
Afloat

Bill Anderson

fernhurst BOOKS

© Fernhurst Books 2002

First published 2002
by Fernhurst Books,
Duke's Path, High Street, Arundel,
West Sussex, BN18 9AJ, England.

British Library Cataloguing in Publication Data.
A catalogue record for this book is available
from the British Library.

ISBN 1 898660 93 X

Printed in Hong Kong through World Print

Acknowledgements
The author and publisher would like to thank:
Garmin for supplying photos of GPS sets and the
screen flowchart;
Sunseeker International for the photo of a
Manhattan 64. Other motorboat pictures
(Chapters 5 and 7) courtesy of Raymarine Ltd;
Farr Yachts for the photo of *Kim*, a Farr 50;
Pickthall Picture Library for the photo of the
Fastnet Rock;
Patrick Roach for all aerial shots of the French
and English coasts;
Casio for the photo of their Pathfinder watch.
Rick Tomlinson for the photo of Disarray.
All other photos by Bill Anderson
and Tim Davison.

Screen dumps by Bill Anderson.

All charts are reproduced from Admiralty charts
by permission of the Controller of Her Majesty's
Stationery Office and the Hydrographic Offices
of France and the UK (www.ukho.gov.uk).

Cover design by Simon Balley.

Design and DTP by Creative Byte.

Contents

Introduction   7

1   Choosing a set   15

2   Getting to work   21

3   Position fixing   31

4   Outputs   41

5   Waypoint navigation   53

6   Passage making   63

7   Pilotage   111

Introduction

This book is for the small boat navigator of the 21st century. Over the last 20 years small boat navigation has undergone a total change. Up until the 1980s the navigator's most difficult problem was to keep track of his position. Decca and Loran went a very long way towards helping him to solve that problem in coastal waters. Now, thanks to GPS, it is no longer a problem anywhere on the world's oceans.

THE GPS SYSTEM

GPS, Global Positioning System to give it its full name, is a satellite position fixing system. It is funded and contolled by the United States Department of Defence for use by the U.S.Military. It is also available, free of charge, to civilian users worldwide.

The system consists of a minimum of 24 operational satellites with orbits arranged so that between five and eight satellites are available at any time to a user anywhere on earth.

Information from three satellites is needed to give a two-dimensional position, four to give height as well.

In very simple terms, GPS works by the satellites transmitting their orbital data and a very accurate time signal. The receiver on your boat measures the time difference between transmission and reception of a signal from a satellite and hence the distance from the satellite. If the system were two dimensional this would give a range circle from each satellite signal but since it is three dimensional it gives a range sphere. The position at which four range spheres intersect is the position of the receiver. As a navigator you really don't need to know any more than that about how the system works but if you are interested there are plenty of excellent web sites which give full information: try searching on 'GPS Navigation'.

When it first became operational the satellite signals available to civilian users were degraded to reduce the positional accuracy of fixes to plus

or minus 200 metres, a process
known as Selective Availability.
In May 2000 Selective Availability
was set to zero, allowing all users to
benefit from the full military system,
giving an accuracy of plus or minus
20 metres.

The current plan for GPS is that it
should continue to be available for
the foreseeable future. There are
plans for improvements to the system
up to the year 2010 and a study is
currently being undertaken to
determine the requirements for
a future generation of satellites.

GPS is widely used for air, marine
and land navigation. Demand for
receivers is huge, allowing
manufacturers to spread their
development costs over long
production runs and hence basic
GPS receivers are very affordable.

With a low user-cost, reliable and
accurate position fixing system
available one might expect stranding
to have become a hazard of the past.

*(Right) GPS is fabulous, but always
double-check your position using
the Mark 1 Eyeball. In this case an
easily-identifiable beacon will
confirm, or give cause to doubt,
the lat. and long. by GPS.*

Surprisingly, the evidence doesn't support this supposition. Lifeboat launches to stranded yachts have actually increased during the time that affordable GPS (and the almost-as-accurate and reliable Decca, which was the system of choice in UK coastal waters prior to the introduction of GPS) has been available. There is little factual information to suggest why this has happened but there are several plausible theories which could account for it. The availability of accurate positional information, which is not degraded by bad weather, poor visibility or darkness, has almost certainly encouraged yachtsmen to undertake more challenging and demanding passages. The fact that positional information, accurate to three places of decimals, is continually available has encouraged a slipshod approach to navigation and fostered an attitude of "I know exactly where I am, why should I bother to navigate?"

Whether either of these theories has any basis of truth is unimportant, the fact remains that neither GPS nor any other electronic position fixing system has replaced the need for careful navigation. The position fixing systems have indeed solved the navigator's traditional problem of "Where am I?" but the human navigator still has to answer two equally important questions, "Is this a safe place to be?" and "Where do I go from here?"

ACCURACY

The limits of accuracy generally quoted for GPS is plus or minus 20 metres. A statistician or scientist will quote percentage deviations and root mean square values which sound impressive but add little to the practical navigator's understanding of the reliance he can place on a position derived from GPS. Accuracy can be further improved by the use of differential GPS, a system in which position by GPS is monitored at a shore station and any differences from the actual position are transmitted to users in the vicinity as corrections to their GPS-derived positions. This brings the accuracy down to the sort of tolerances needed to slot an oil supply pipe onto an offshore wellhead 20 metres under the North Sea. The currently available differential systems are operated on a national basis and sets which can make use of differential signals are considerably more expensive than those which can not. A new differential system, Wide Area Augmentation System (WAAS), which should give accuracy of three to five metres, was undergoing trials in the USA in 2001 and was expected to become generally available there within a couple of years. New sets with the ability to make use of WAAS are already available and similar systems are being developed for Europe and Japan.

While the GPS system may be capable of delivering exceptional accuracy this does not always mean that the user can rely on navigating to those limits. GPS is the most accurate world-wide position fixing system we have ever enjoyed and the very accuracy of the system has brought its own problems. The charts on which we navigate are compiled from surveys carried out over the last two centuries. Many of them are based on local or regional datums which themselves depended on astronomical observations taken with instruments of previous generations. The GPS system itself is based on WGS84, and navigational charts produced by the major national hydrographic offices are being redrawn on the WGS84 datum or on a datum which is so close to WGS84 that any small differences are of no practical significance. However, we will continue to navigate on charts based on other datums for many years so we need to understand their significance.

When using charts based on other datums, such as the Ordnance Survey of Great Britain 1936 (OSGB36) datum on which most UK charts are drawn, it is possible to reset the GPS receiver to that datum. Our European neighbours use other datums, such as the European 1950 (ED50) and it is fatally easy to move onto a chart based on a different datum which can induce significant errors in GPS positions. For instance, if we are lying in berth F38 in Trebeurden marina on the North Brittany coast and plot our position on the largest scale French chart, based on ED50, with the GPS set to ED50, the position given is within a few metres of the correct berth. On switching the GPS receiver to OSGB36 the position moves SSW some 190 metres and we now appear to be on the edge of the car park. Switching the GPS receiver to WGS84 brings us to an indicated position 130 metres SW of our actual berth, just outside the sea wall. These are typical of the magnitude of error which will be introduced by failing to notice that the chart on which you are navigating is based on a different datum from the one to which the GPS is set.

If you are navigating on an old chart, or even a chart based on old surveys, you may find that even though you have set your GPS for the right datum you still seem to be getting positions which are substantially in error. In fact it is not your position which is in error, it is the charted positions of the land which are wrong.

A couple of seasons sailing with GPS, particularly in an area with accurate up-to-date charts can lead to a high degree of confidence in the system, to the extent that it is treated as a complete navigation system and not just an aid to navigation. The Royal Navy navigation school used to maintain details of the twenty most expensive British warship groundings, which were used as cautionary tales for budding navigators. The common theme running through them all was that up to the moment that the keel hit the rock, sand or mud, the Captain and his Navigating Officer knew exactly where the ship was, or at least they thought they did. Navigational disaster is seldom anything to do with getting lost, because once there is an element of doubt in the navigator's mind he becomes extra

cautious and double checks on his position. Disaster strikes when he is arrogant enough to be totally convinced, beyond a shadow of doubt, that he has the navigational situation totally under control, even though his assumed position is based on just one set of data which he has not bothered to cross-check against anything else. It is a frame of mind all too easily encouraged by the accuracy and reliability of GPS.

YOUR GPS

This book is a guide to the basics of navigation by GPS. It does not attempt to replace the user manual for your particular set, because different manufacturers have slightly different terminology for the operation of their sets and different models provide different user controls and varying levels of sophistication. To master the controls and find out exactly what the set will or will not do there is no alternative to reading the manual.

1 Choosing a set

Fig 1.1 A typical hand-held set.

There is no shortage of choice when it comes to buying a GPS. There are several manufacturers, all producing a range of different models. They all function and as long as you don't decide to scour the boat jumble sales for something second-hand it would be difficult to buy a dud.

Most manufacturers produce three levels of set: hand-held, fixed and combined GPS/chart plotter. Within each level there are varying degrees of sophistication in the outputs offered.

The hand-helds (Fig 1.1) tend to be the least expensive. They operate from their own internal dry batteries, typically four AA alkaline, giving a battery life of anything up to 24 hours. Most can also operate from the boat's 12 volt supply through a cigar lighter connection. They have an internal aerial, again with the option to connect to an external one. Their controls are likely to be up to six individual function keys and up, down, left and right arrow keys.

Hand-helds are ideal for boats in which there is no secure stowage

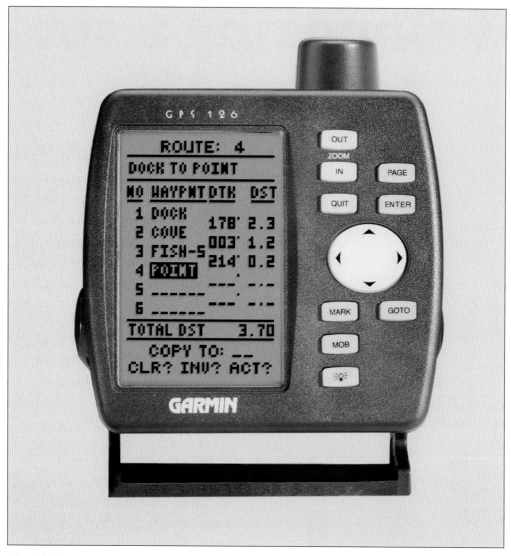

Fig 1.2 A typical fixed set.

for a fixed set. Their advantages include low cost, small size and portability. The main disadvantages from which they tend to suffer are cramped controls and a small screen, which can be difficult to read. Without an external aerial they may also have difficulty tracking satellites from inside a yacht, at the chart table for instance, because the yacht's structure screens the aerial from the satellite signals. If they are left switched on they use batteries at quite a rate so it makes sense to turn them off when not actually needed for navigation. This means that the set is not immediately available for use: it takes a few minutes to find the satellites each time it is switched on.

A hand-held is also extremely useful if you are sailing short-handed or if you are prone to seasickness if you have to go below. You can use it in the cockpit without the need to go to the chart table to change screens or settings.

Some hand-helds are designed primarily for walkers and include map displays designed for land expeditions.

The ultimate, so far, in portables is the wristwatch style of GPS. You need a large wrist to wear one with any degree of comfort and they suffer from tiny controls and a very small screen size, but as a Christmas present for the man who has everything...

Fixed sets (Fig 1.2) are generally larger than hand-helds. This allows them to have more controls or more space between the controls, which makes them easier to use, and larger screens which are easier to read. Most of them have remote aerials which can be mounted clear of obstructions to avoid any masking of satellites. They can be connected to remote screens so that a display is available both at the chart table and at the steering position. Most offer the ability to interface the

GPS with a personal computer, chart plotter or autopilot.

Combined GPS/chart plotters (Fig 1.3) are available at a variety of levels of sophistication. The most useful for marine navigation operate from navigational charts stored on cartridges or disks. These come in a range of sizes and can hold the data for areas that would typically be covered by anything between a large scale Admiralty chart up to an area that would be covered by several dozen charts. Many combined GPS/chart plotters suffer from relatively small displays, which make it difficult to show sufficient area of chart at a convenient scale.

The cost of electronic chart coverage for an area is broadly similar to the cost of paper charts. However, since navigators are by nature cautious and conservative there is a great reluctance to rely entirely on electronic charts so they tend to be an addition to – rather than a replacement for – paper charts.

Do not confuse marine chart plotters with the map displays which are available, in varying degrees of sophistication, on many hand-helds. These range from a basic track plotter which shows a representation of the track followed, to street maps for vehicle or pedestrian navigation.

Fig 1.3 A combined GPS/ colour chart plotter.

Both have their uses but these do not include navigation at sea.

Marine chart plotters which display full navigational charts can be interfaced to most fixed and some hand-held sets and they are an excellent method of displaying chart information, including your position on the chart. They can operate either with Raster charts, which are exact dot-for-dot copies of paper charts, or with Vector charts, which allow layers of information to be displayed or hidden, ridding the screen of unwanted information and producing a much clearer picture.

The other device which is included under the generic title of electronic plotters is the Yeoman Chart Plotter. This consists of a chart board on which the chart is placed and referenced.

The plotter 'puck' will then, when placed on the chart, give a reading of latitude and longitude or, if supplied with a lat. and long. position from the GPS, make it easy to plot your position by moving the puck across the chart until the lit arrows go out.

Buying a GPS is rather like buying a new computer: no matter when you buy it you inevitably find that a new model with more features appears on the market two days after you bought yours. This is life, don't worry about it. There was a temptation to delay the purchase of GPS because prices were falling and next month the model you wanted would cost 10% less. Those days seem to have gone, the economies of scale which came with an expanding market have now been fully absorbed and prices are now more or less keeping pace with inflation.

If you are buying your first GPS you will find a confusingly wide range available. Your budget and the type of boat you use should narrow down the choice considerably. It is then just a matter of playing with demonstration sets at boat shows to find which one has the screen and control layouts which you like best. It is very much a matter of personal preference and it really is as simple as that.

Fig 1.4 The Casio Pathfinder watch. The rechargeable battery gives one hour of continuous GPS measurement, or 70 individual GPS measurements (plus time).

2 Getting to work

INSTALLATION

Most fixed GPS sets are relatively easy to install and whether you undertake the job yourself or have it done for you is a matter of whether you run your boat on a DIY or full professional support basis. Whichever you do, you will have to decide where you want it mounted. The key to making the right choice is to think about how you are going to use it and there are two conflicting requirements which you will have to satisfy.

Much use of the GPS will be at the chart table, where you will do the passage planning, entering waypoints and

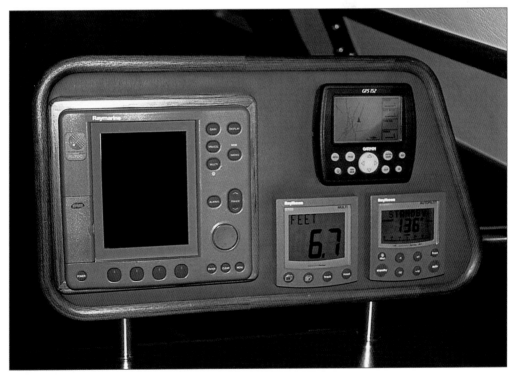

Fig 2.1 Navigation instruments installed at the chart table, including radar, GPS, echo sounder and log.

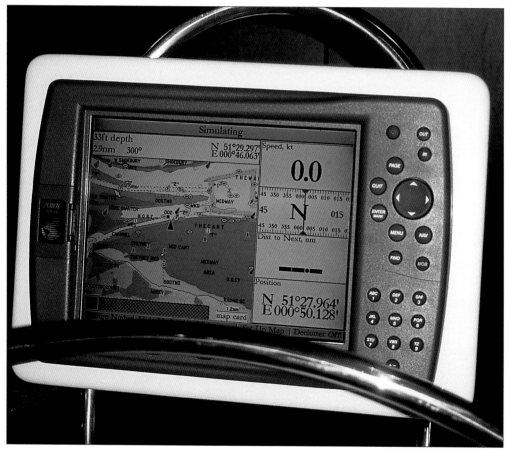

Fig 2.2 A colour chart plotter installed perfectly for viewing by the helmsperson.

routes and where you will also transfer positions from the GPS screen to the chart (Fig 2.1). But it is also highly likely that the helmsman or watch keeper will want to refer to the GPS from the cockpit or steering position. For this to be possible the GPS must be mounted in a position where it is visible from the cockpit (out of the question with some chart table layouts) or it must be connected to a remote readout which can be positioned in an instrument bank above the companionway or on the steering pedestal (Fig 2.2).

If you are installing a set with a remote aerial you also have to decide where you are going to site the aerial. The only criteria to meet are that it should have as clear a view of the sky as possible, it should not be vulnerable to damage by flailing sheets or flogging sails and it should not present itself as a convenient handhold to crew members

Fig 2.3 Mount the aerial where it has a clear view of the sky but where it won't be grabbed by the crew. The pushpit is ideal.

or visitors coming on board. It does not have to be mounted high up, in fact a masthead installation would not be good because the motion of the aerial in a seaway would confuse the computation of speed and direction made good. The site of choice in a sailing boat is usually on the stern rail (Fig 2.3) or an aerial gantry and on a motorboat the top of the superstructure.

USER CONTROLS

Very few GPS sets have full alphanumeric keypads: they rely on relatively few user controls, each of which performs a number of functions (Fig 2.4). If you are a regular user of a computer and a mobile phone the conventions used on GPS controls and in user handbooks should present few

Goes to waypoints list to allow user to select active waypoint.

Moves to the next display.

The On/Off switch, also switches on screen lighting.

Establishes a waypoint at the present position.

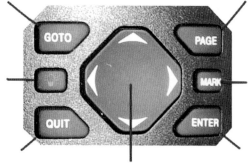

Returns to the previous page.

Activates a highlighted field to allow data entry and confirms data entry

The arrow keys
Move the cursor up and down, or left and right, on screen. Up and down used to increase or decrease the value of a digit highlighted by the cursor.

Fig 2.4 Typical user controls.

problems and you can skip the rest of this section, just read your user handbook. If you don't use a computer and you struggle to send text messages on a mobile phone then you have some learning to do about the use of left/right and up/down arrows and scrolling menus.

Very few of the user controls have a unique function, what they actually do depends on what is displayed on the screen. To take a very simple example, one major manufacturer's models have nothing labelled as an on/off key, you turn the set on by pressing a key marked with a light bulb and hold it pressed until something appears on the screen. The same key is then used, by pressing it briefly, to switch the back-lighting on and off and it is also used, by holding it pressed for three seconds, to switch the set off. All very simple once you know about it, but the point it illustrates is that trying to figure out the user controls without reference to the instruction manual is a mug's game .

There are some important jargon words that you need to become

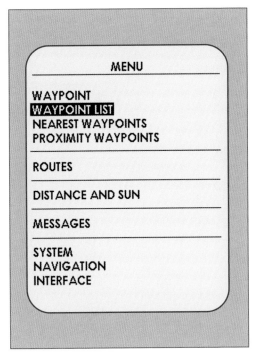

Fig 2.5 Typical menu screen.

familiar with. The most important are:

Cursor. The highlighted section of the screen, indicating which field, letter or number can be changed.

Field. A part of the screen where a word or string of digits can be entered.

Menu. A list of options (Fig 2.5).

The left/right and up/down arrow keys take the place of an alphanumeric keypad. When you need to enter numbers or letters on the screen the left/right arrows allow you to move from one letter or number to the next (right arrow) or to the previous one (left arrow). The up/down arrows allow you to increase or decrease the value of the letter or number highlighted by the cursor. For instance, if you want to enter the letter D, press the up arrow and you will see the letter change from A to B to C to D. If you want the letter X it is easier to go in from the other end of the alphabet by using the down key, progressing through Z and Y to X. (Going in from the end of the alphabet you will probably have to go through 9,8,7,6, 5,4,3,2,1,0, before you come to Z but it is still quicker than starting at A). It seems to be a tediously time-consuming exercise at first but speed improves greatly with practice.

GPS user handbooks talk about menus , sub-menus, pop-up menus and pages. These are all jargon for a standard layout of information on the screen. Most sets have one or more controls which allow you to change from one set of information to another. This often has to be done by moving through the information sets in a predetermined order, just like turning the pages of a book. Many manufacturers produce an extremely useful card (Fig 2.6) which illustrates the order in which the menus appear and the key which has to be pressed to

O P E R A T I O N　F L O W C H A R T

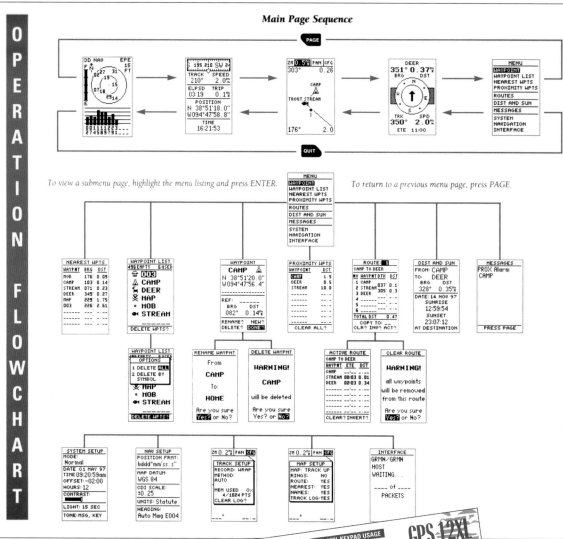

Main Page Sequence

To view a submenu page, highlight the menu listing and press ENTER.　　　To return to a previous menu page, press PAGE.

Fig 2.6 Sample card illustrating sequence of menus.

move between them. It is a good idea to have this card permanently mounted on the bulkhead by the chart table.

INITIALISATION AND SETUP

Initialisation and setup are actually two totally different processes but a number of sets combine them in a single menu.

Initialisation is the process of switching on the set and putting it into operation for the first time. Some sets do it automatically, others require an approximate position to be entered by the user. The set then takes a few minutes to sort out the satellite information it is receiving before it starts to operate. Most sets will require re-initialising if they have been moved more than 500 miles while switched off.

Setup is the process of setting the outputs to the units, references and formats which you want to use (Fig 2.7). There are several which are important. All have default settings, which will be used if you do nothing about them. We have already mentioned datums. Most sets will use WGS 84 as the default setting. Most Admiralty charts of the UK are based on the Ordnance Survey of Great Britain 1936 but are currently (2002) being changed to a datum which is for all practical

purposes identical to WGS 84. Whenever you use a new chart for the first time you need to check the datum, which is usually given under the title. Changing the datum of your set is easy, you just have to remember to do it.

The default position output is usually latitude and longitude, in degrees and minutes to three decimal places, and this is the simplest to use. Degrees, minutes and seconds; degrees to several places of decimals; and several land survey grids are usually also available but there is no particular reason to use any of them.

Nautical miles are the usual default setting for distance. Statute miles and kilometres are commonly available alternatives but again there is no reason to use them for marine navigation.

If your set has a Highway style of display you will be able to specify the width of highway you want displayed.

Heading and bearing references can be either true or magnetic north. In a yacht with magnetic steering and hand bearing compasses most of the other information you use will be magnetic so this is the obvious setting for the GPS. If you are selecting magnetic you may be given the option simply to specify 'Magnetic', in which

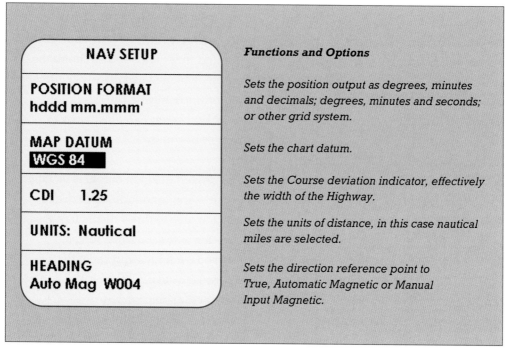

NAV SETUP	Functions and Options
POSITION FORMAT hddd mm.mmm'	Sets the position output as degrees, minutes and decimals; degrees, minutes and seconds; or other grid system.
MAP DATUM WGS 84	Sets the chart datum.
CDI 1.25	Sets the Course deviation indicator, effectively the width of the Highway.
UNITS: Nautical	Sets the units of distance, in this case nautical miles are selected.
HEADING Auto Mag W004	Sets the direction reference point to True, Automatic Magnetic or Manual Input Magnetic.

Fig 2.7 Navigation setup screen.

case the set will apply the variation – stored in its database - for the present position, or you can enter the variation, east or west, which you wish to use.

The GPS time reference is Universal Time or UT (for those who like old measure, this is the same as Greenwich Mean Time or GMT) but you can usually change the display to local time and it is generally convenient to do so.

Most sets have several alarms which you can set. Typically they might include:

- **Arrival.** The distance, or in some cases time at present speed, from a waypoint at which you want an alarm to sound.
- **Anchor drag.** When this is set, you can decide what displacement from the anchorage position you will allow before the alarm sounds. Don't forget to allow a reasonable swinging circle.
- **Off Track.** The distance off track at which you want an alarm to sound.

Other settings include general housekeeping items such as the level of contrast, brightness and length of time to sustain background

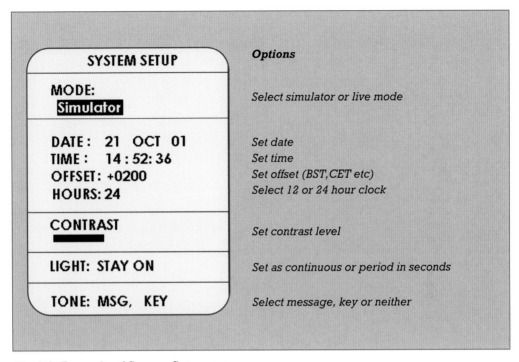

Fig 2.8 Example of System Setup menu.

lighting, and alarm tones - which are largely a matter of personal preference (Fig 2.8). But it you are using a hand-held set on internal batteries do not be tempted to leave the background lighting on for longer than you need or you will radically shorten the battery life .

At least one manufacturer provides a security coding, just like the security code in the more expensive car radios, but you enter it yourself during the set-up procedure. If you activate the code you have to enter it every time you switch on the set - entering the wrong code causes the set to shut down and prevents its use. If you feel that you need this sort of protection against theft by all means set the code. I wouldn't use one myself: the possibility of a memory lapse at the vital moment when the set is being switched on in an emergency is too horrific to contemplate.

3 Position fixing

Many people buying their first GPS do so with the attitude that they don't want a lot of fancy extras, they just want something that will tell them where they are. Position fixing is indeed a useful function of GPS but to regard it as the primary function would be to miss the point of what GPS can do for you.

THE NAVIGATOR'S GRID - LATITUDE AND LONGITUDE

For at least half a century before we started using electronic position fixing systems we navigated by drawing, so the end result of the position-finding process was a dot or a cross actually drawn on the chart. The next stage was to draw a line from where we were to our destination, which gave us a course to make good and from that it was relatively simple to work out a course to steer. With electronics the basic position we are given is a grid reference, usually expressed as a latitude and longitude. Once we have a position we can ask the machine for a course to another

latitude and longitude and it will oblige. There is, at least in theory, no need to refer to the chart.

The change actually completes a full circle in navigational technique, taking us back to the days before accurate navigational charts, when the navigator worked out, by a laborious tabular process or by spherical trigonometry, the course and distance to his destination. The essential difference between the navigational techniques of today and those of a century ago is that we have the benefit of a computer built into our position fixing device which gives instant answers to course to destination and distance to go problems which took our predecessors hours to calculate.

Anyone using an electronic position fixing system needs to be totally familiar with using latitude and longitude and its application as a reference grid on charts.

The overall system is shown in fig 3.1. The parallels of latitude, coloured red on the diagram, start with the equator, which is zero. They are then measured

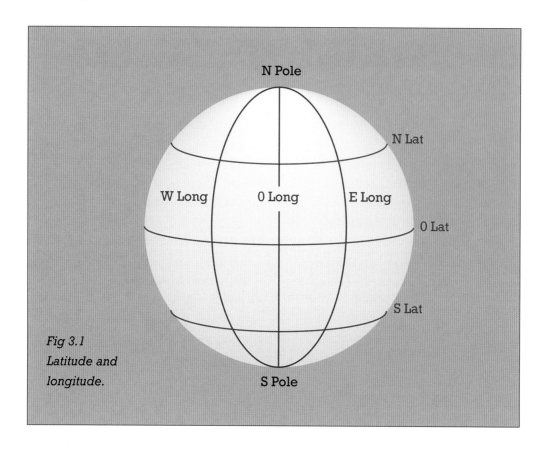

Fig 3.1
Latitude and
longitude.

north and south to the poles, the north pole is 90° north, the south pole 90° south. 50° north runs through the middle of the English Channel. The latitude of any point on the earth is its angular measurement, north or south from the equator, as shown in Fig 3.2 .

The meridians of longitude, shown in blue in Fig 3.3, are measured east and west from the Greenwich meridian, so that the maximum possible east or west longitude is 180°, which corresponds approximately with the International Date Line.

Both latitude and longitude are usually expressed in degrees, minutes and decimals of a minute and should always be named, north or south for latitude, east or west for longitude. There are 60 minutes in a degree. (You may occasionally come across a latitude or longitude expressed in degrees, minutes and seconds, with 60 seconds in a minute, but this is unusual in navigation.)

By convention, a latitude of 25 degrees 20.5 minutes north is written as 25° 20'.5N. GPS screens adopt a slightly

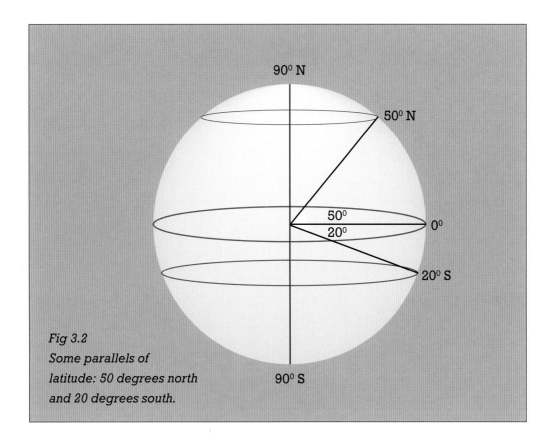

Fig 3.2
Some parallels of
latitude: 50 degrees north
and 20 degrees south.

different convention: they would show this as N25°20.500'.

The latitude scale on a chart also gives a distance scale, with one minute of latitude representing one sea mile. When using a chart drawn on a Mercator projection the latitude scale is not constant so it is important to use the part of the latitude scale which is as nearly as possible at the same latitude as the distance to be measured. The smaller the scale of the chart the more important this becomes. Try it on the smallest scale mercator chart you can

lay hands on, open your dividers to an exact number of minutes of latitude at the northern end of the latitude scale and see what this corresponds to at the southern end of the scale. You will find that there is a significant difference.

For all practical purposes you can assume that a sea mile and a nautical mile are identical.

The longitude scale cannot be used as a means of measuring distance. One minute of longitude at the equator is approximately equal to a nautical

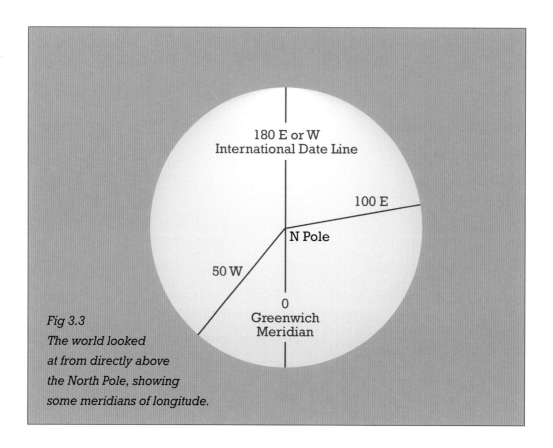

Fig 3.3

The world looked at from directly above the North Pole, showing some meridians of longitude.

mile, but as you move north or south away from the equator the length of a minute of longitude progressively decreases, reaching zero at the pole.

The conventional form for giving the latitude and longitude of a position is to give the latitude first, followed by the longitude. For example, Channel Light Vessel is at 49° 54'.5N 002° 53'.2W.

Most GPS sets give you the option of different formats for lat. and long, either degrees, minutes and decimals of a minute or degrees, minutes and

seconds, with the former as the default setting. GPS displays are, like most computer-based devices, absolutely inflexible in the format, and the position of the Channel Light Vessel would be shown on a typical display as:

N   49° 54.500'

W 002° 53.200'

How you plot and take off positions as lat. and long. on a chart is very much a matter of personal preference. I find it easiest to plot a position by laying off the lat. with a plotting instrument, drawing a short pencil line and then

Plotting position on the chart by latitude and longitude (Fig 3.4)

1. Open the dividers to the required longitude, working from the top or bottom edge of the chart.

2. Find the correct latitude on the left or right hand scale. Use a plotter or parallel rule to lay off the latitude (draw a pencil line).

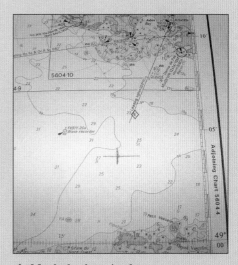

3. Using dividers, lay off the longitude at the marked latitude.

4. Mark the longitude. The cross is your position.

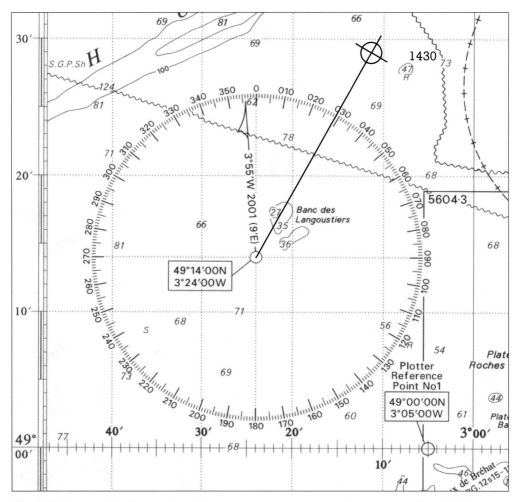

Fig 3.5 If you make the centre of a compass rose a waypoint you can plot a fix by range and bearing from that waypoint.

striking off the long. with a pair of dividers (Fig 3.4). Taking positions off the chart I use the dividers for both lat. and long.. I wouldn't claim any particular merit for this way of working, it just happens to suit me.

So much for a quick revision of the basics of lat. and long.. No apologies to anyone who thought that any aspiring satellite navigator should know all that. Many years ago a famous yachtsman was making a single-handed circumnavigation, sending daily reports to the press of position and distance run. Everything seemed logical until the great adventurer rounded the Cape of Good Hope, after which the claimed daily distances run began to far exceed the actual distances between daily position reports. The cause of the discrepancy was eventually pinned down to the navigator, on starting to travel east instead of south, measuring progress from the longitude instead of the latitude scale. The basics really are important and we can all get them wrong.

POSITION FIXING

When you have been using GPS for a while you will be tempted to do all your navigation relative to waypoints and to ignore the basic lat. and long. output completely. Resist the temptation. The lat. and long. output is the only one which does not depend on some reference point which you have chosen and input to the set. It is inevitable that you will occasionally make a mistake in the definition or input of a waypoint and if all your navigation is with reference to that point it will make perfect sense, with plausible distances run between fixes but it will all be in error by the amount of the error in the waypoint position.

The purpose of taking a fix and plotting the yacht's position on the chart is seldom just to find out where you are - very often you can see just by looking round at landmarks roughly where you are. The purpose of formally going through the process of marking the precise position on the chart is to make sure that you have not misidentified a mark, that you aren't standing into danger, or travelling in the wrong direction. The whole process of fixing your position and plotting it on the chart is part of the routine of keeping the yacht safe. (A traditionalist may tell you that you need regular fixes to monitor your course and speed over the ground but in fact the GPS will tell you that much more accurately than you can work it out by measuring the direction and distance between fixes plotted on the chart.)

In visual navigation we are taught to take and plot three bearings. Two bearings could actually give us as accurate a position as three. The third position line adds nothing to the accuracy, it probably results in a triangle rather than a single cross on the chart. But what the third position line does is to help us to check that we haven't made a gross error, because if we have we will get a huge 'Cocked Hat'. We then know that we have to ditch that fix and start again.

GPS is never going to give you a position which is grossly in error but there is always the possibility that you will transpose digits and make

a significant error in the plotting.
The resulting fix is going to be just
a cross on the chart, there is no third
position line to alert you to an error.
All the usual cross-checks are still
important, or even more important,
when navigating with GPS. Keep an
Estimated Position (EP) on the chart
and compare the fix with the EP, check
the depth by echo sounder with the
charted depth and have a good look
round to check that any landmarks tie
in with the fix position.

If you are plotting fixes by lat. and
long. you can make your life easier by
thinking about how you fold the chart
to fit on the chart table, so that both
a lat. and a long. scale are visible.
It is also particularly important to
keep the charts tidy and not have
more than one on the chart table at
a time, otherwise you risk using a lat.
or long. scale from another chart,
protruding from under the one actually
in use.

One way to make it easier to plot fixes
is to enter the centre of the nearest
compass rose as a waypoint. Then
instead of plotting lat. and long. you
can plot bearing and range of the
waypoint, which is a much simpler
process (Fig 3.5). Each Admiralty Small
Craft chart now shows the lat. and long.
of the centre of each compass rose,
which makes this even easier, although

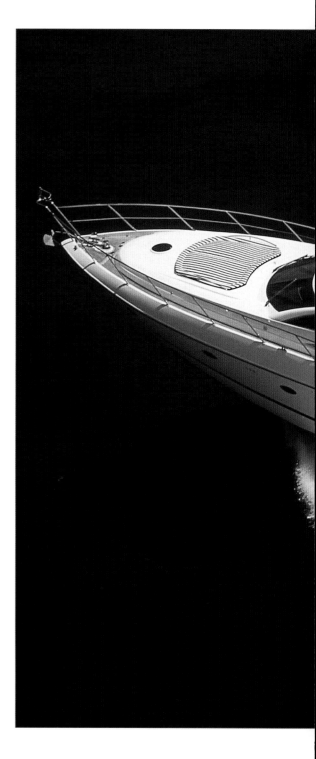

In boats capable of very high speeds there is little time for chartwork at sea so thorough planning is essential.

the roses are based on true north, so if you have your GPS set to magnetic you do have to convert from magnetic to true before plotting the position.

Be careful that you do not allow the ease of finding your position with an electronic system to lull you into a sense of false security. At least one yacht has simply sailed into a cliff on a dark night because her skipper knew he could easily plot a position whenever he wanted to, he just didn't bother to until it was too late. As a general rule you need to check your position often enough for this to be impossible, i.e. if you are close to the coast and on a course which is converging on an invisible hazard, take and plot fixes at least often enough to detect impending disaster if your helmsman is steering a rather approximate course or the stream might set you inshore. It is not sensible to have a rule of thumb such as plot a fix every 15 minutes; in mid-ocean once a day may be quite enough, but skirting the edge of a sandbank 15 minute intervals could be too long.

4 Outputs

GPS receiver software designers have come up with a number of ingenious ways of presenting information on the screen. The ones available on your set will be described in the user's handbook. It is important to know what the displays can and cannot do to help you. As an example of the typical outputs available I have based most of the examples on the Garmin 126 (abbreviated to G126 for reference purposes) to illustrate a typical range.

THE SATELLITE SCREEN

This gives a representation of the satellites available for navigation and the signal strengths from each of them (Fig 4.1). On most sets some indication is also given of Dilution of Precision (DoP), Accuracy or Estimated Position Error (EPE). This is a measure of how good the geometry of the satellites is for position fixing. If it is shown as DoP

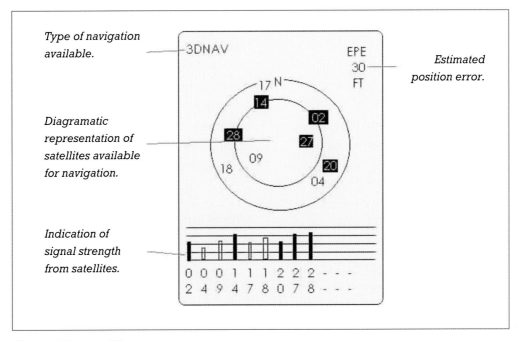

Fig 4.1 The satellite screen.

the lower the number the better the geometry. The Accuracy or EPE figure is an estimate of the likely inaccuracy of position fixes, expressed as a distance in feet or metres from the true position. The figure is almost always encouragingly small but it is not an absolute guarantee that the error of your position will not exceed that figure, it is just a statement that the inaccuracy is unlikely to exceed it. All in all this is not an output that is going to be of much practical significance in yacht navigation, better really to work on a likely positional accuracy to within 20 metres.

The top left hand corner of this screen is used in the G126 to indicate the receiver status, using the following jargon:

1 **Searching.** Looking for available satellites.
2 **Autolocate.** Collecting new almanac data.
3 **Acquiring.** Collecting data from satellites but does not yet have enough to calculate a position.
4 **2D Nav.** Locked on to at least 3 satellites with good geometry and is calculating a 2-dimensional fix.
5 **3D Nav.** Locked on to at least 4 satellites with good geometry and is calculating a 3-dimensional fix.
6 **Poor GPS Coverage**. Not tracking enough satellites for a fix.
7 **Not Usable.** The receiver is

unusable, possibly due to abnormal satellite conditions. Turn off and on again to reset the receiver.
8 **Simulator.** The receiver is in simulator mode.

In my experience, messages 6 and 7 are extremely rare. The satellite geometry is usually good and loss of lock occurs very rarely, typically only when the aerial's view of the sky is obstructed. On most sets, if GPS coverage or the received signal becomes poor an alarm sounds, a warning message is diplayed and information fields such as Course and Speed Made Good go blank. On a few older sets the warnings are less clear and it is possible to continue to read data from the screen when it is displaying nothing more useful than the data it had at the time it lost lock on the satellites. Failure to notice that the receiver was no longer updating position from the satellites caused the stranding of a cruise liner off the east coast of the USA some years ago, much to the embarrassment of her operators.

THE POSITION SCREEN

This is a really useful screen (Fig 4.2). On nearly all sets it gives position as lat. and long., Course and Speed Over the Ground, Altitude and Time. On some sets the Course Over the Ground

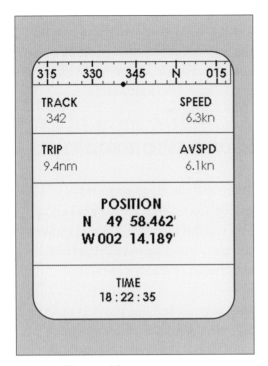

Fig 4.2 The position screen.

is shown as some form of diagrammatic compass. While this can be helpful as a visual representation of direction travelled it is important to remember that it is not a representation of heading so it cannot be used as a heading reference to steer by.

While GPS accuracy in the horizontal plane is excellent for marine navigation, the same claim cannot be made for its indication of height. Do not be tempted to use this output as even the crudest estimate of height of tide. The claimed system accuracy for height is plus or minus 27 metres which is a long way from the sort of

limits to which we need to know tidal heights!

The G126 provides two user-selectable fields on this screen which can be chosen from:

1 **Trip (TRIP).** Distance travelled since last reset, the equivalent of log reading but it gives distance over the ground rather than distance through the water.
2 **Trip timer (TTIME).** The total time for which a ground speed has been maintained since last reset.
3 **Elapsed Time (ELPSD).** Hours and minutes since last reset.
4 **Average Speed (AVSPD).** Average speed travelled.
5 **Maximum Speed (MXSPD).** Maximum speed since last reset.
6 **Altitude (ALT).** Vertical distance above sea level.

Of the six, 1 and 4 are probably the most useful. If you know what average speed you have to maintain to arrive at a tidal gate then 4 can tell you whether or not you are keeping up to schedule, although it cannot tell you whether changes in tidal stream between now and the time of arrival at the gate are going to help or hinder. Maximum speed is fun to have for competitions between helmsmen or between watches to see who can achieve the highest ground speed during a passage or a cruise.

THE MAP OR PLOTTER SCREEN

This is a map-style screen which shows the track followed and the locations of surrounding waypoints (Fig 4.3). On more sophisticated sets it may have a database of navigational aids which appear on the map and it may have a pointer device which allows you to measure range and bearing of selected positions. There are options to change the range of the display, to 'pan' to different areas, to show range circles and to orientate the display Track Up or North Up. There is also a 'pointer' which can be used to measure the bearing and distance to a waypoint or

to any part of the screen. In general, the basic map pages have always seemed to me to be more of a gimmick than a useful navigational tool.

NAVIGATION SCREENS

There are two common forms of navigation screen, the Compass (Fig 4.4) and the Highway (Fig 4.5). Either can be used when navigating towards a waypoint or along a route.

Both of these screens provide bearing and distance to the active waypoint and Course and Speed Made Good over the ground. This information is

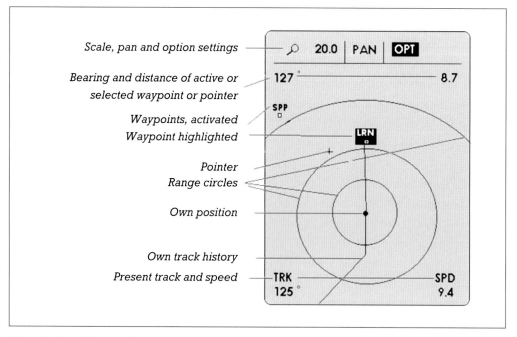

Fig 4.3 The Map or Plotter Screen.

shown at the top of the screen. At the bottom of the screen there are two items of information, which can be selected from:

1 **Estimated Time Enroute (ETE).** The time it will take to reach the active waypoint at the present speed made good.

2 **Estimated Time of Arrival (ETA).** The time at which you will arrive at the active waypoint at the present speed made good.

3 **Course To Steer (CTS).** The bearing which will give you the most efficient way to stay on course to your destination.

4 **Crosstrack Error (XTK).** The distance you are off the track from your starting point to the active waypoint. On the highway screen this is also shown graphically on the course deviation indicator (CDI).

5 **Velocity Made Good (VMG).** The speed at which you are travelling in the direction of the active waypoint.

6 **Turn (TRN).** The amount of course correction you need to make, in degrees left or right, to travel directly towards the active waypoint.

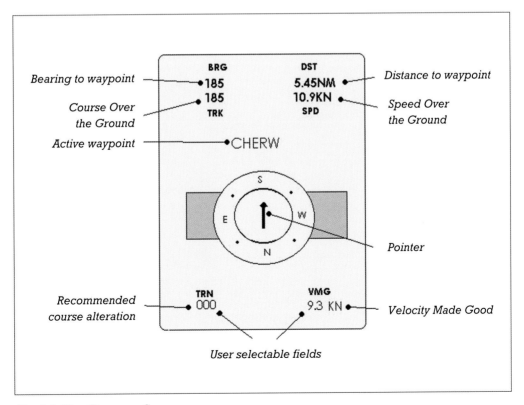

Fig 4.4 The Compass Screen.

All of these information items can be useful but most of them can also be misleading if they are misused. 1 and 2 do exactly what their definition says, but if you are more than a few miles from your destination, particularly in a sailing boat, it is highly unlikely that you will maintain the present speed made good for the whole passage. Hence you are unlikely to arrive at the active waypoint exactly at the time predicted by the GPS; you have to do the calculation yourself, making allowance for changes in tidal streams and forecast changes in wind direction and strength.

Item 3 is an indication of a course to steer which will get you back onto the direct line from your starting point to the next waypoint. On a long passage it is likely to be unhelpful because you probably do not want to stay on the direct line, you will have calculated a single Course To Steer which will result in being carried quite a long way off track and then back again when the tide turns.

Item 4 is an extremely useful one. On many passages you will know how much safe water there is on

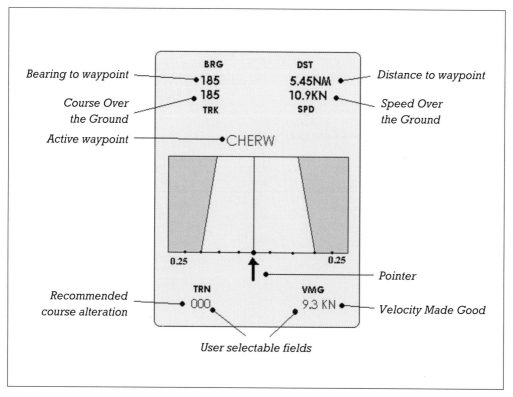

Fig 4.5 The Highway Screen.

each side of your planned track and the Crosstrack Error allows you to monitor progress in such a way that you avoid leaving the planed line by more than your known safety margin.

Item 5, VMG, is particularly useful in a sailing boat on a windward passage because it tells you how fast you are going towards your destination. As you move away from the directly down-wind line from the destination the VMG will start to drop. When you tack, it should increase. If you have a strong cross-tide, working out which

is the more favourable tack is quite a complicated exercise but a quick trial and error session on each tack will very quickly show which gives the higher VMG and hence is the more advantageous.

In the centre of the screen you have the option of the Compass or the Highway Display. The Highway Display uses the slope of the Highway to show which way you should steer to regain the track. In the situation illustrated (Fig 4.6) you are to port of track and need to alter course to starboard in order to regain

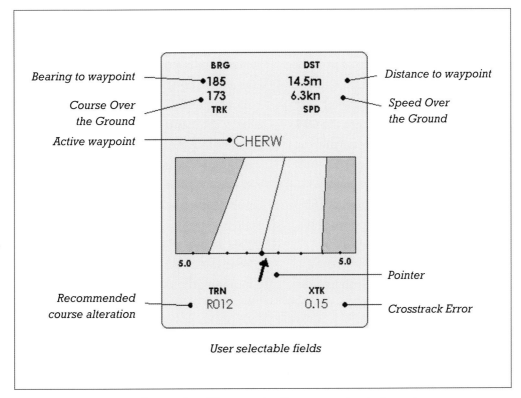

Fig 4.6 The Highway Screen is telling you to alter course to starboard.

the track. The Crosstrack Error (XTK) shows that you are 0.15 miles off track. This information is all concerned with where you are in relation to the line from your starting point to your destination.

A further set of figures tells you which way you are moving and suggests the action you need to take to move towards the waypoint. The Course Over the Ground figure (TRK) shows that you are actually moving in the direction 173°, and the recommended course alteration (TRN) tells you that you need to alter course 12° to starboard to head directly towards the waypoint. Nothing on the GPS screen tells you in what direction your boat is actually pointing; to find that out you have to look at the steering compass. Assuming that you are actually steering a course of 185° the information coming from the GPS suggests that the tidal stream and/or leeway is setting you 12° to port and if you alter course 12° to starboard you will make good a course of 185° directly towards the waypoint. The Pointer, the arrow just below the highway, gives an indication of the direction of the waypoint relative to the direction in which you are moving.

If this all seems slightly confusing, it is probably because the display is presenting you with two different sets of information. The first consists of

Crosstrack error (XTK), Course to steer (CTS) and the slope of the highway, which are about the side of the line from starting point to destination that you are and how to return to that line. The second, Course over the ground (TRK), Turn (TRN), and the direction of the Pointer, tell you about the direction in which you are moving and what you might do to adjust your heading so that you move directly towards your destination.

Let us look at a slightly different situation on the highway screen (Fig 4.7). The only three fields which have changed, outlined in grey, are the Course Over the Ground, the Turn and the Pointer. The boat in this case is moving in the direction 200°, as shown by the TRK figure, the recommended course alteration is 15° to port and the Pointer now shows that the waypoint is to port of the direction in which the boat is moving. She is still 0.15 miles to port of the track.

This screen could well arise if the helmsman had wandered off course momentarily or if the boat was steering well to starboard of the waypoint in order to regain the track.

The Highway Screen is most useful when there are dangers to be avoided on one or both sides of the track, and it is helpful to have a continuous indication of which side of the track you are and of how far off it you are.

With the Compass version of the navigation page (Fig 4.8) you have a slightly different set of data. This is exactly the same situation as the last Highway Screen we looked at but the emphasis is now on the direction in which the boat is moving. The display of Crosstrack Error in the bottom right hand field is virtually meaningless because it tells us how far off track we are but does not tell us to which

side. It would be more sensible to display a different user-selectable field here, such as ETA.

It is perfectly possible to do all your navigation by reference to the navigation screens, the marine equivalent of flying on instruments. Assuming that you make sensible passage plans, 99 times out of 100 you will arrive safely at your destination with no more than a cursory glance at the chart while at sea. Sailing short handed, particularly in bad weather, the navigation screens do allow you

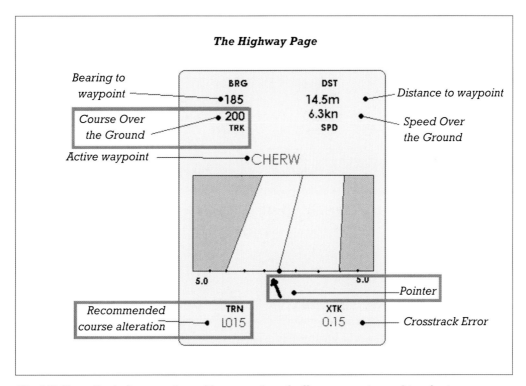

Fig 4.7 Here the helmsman has either wandered off course or turned too far to starboard. The boat is still 0.15 miles to port of the Track. See text for a full explanation.

to monitor progress with the minimum of effort and hence they greatly increase your overall safety. However, it is possible to navigate yourself into bad trouble with them by misreading an output, by navigating with reference to the wrong waypoint or by making an error when entering a waypoint position. Hence you do need to follow the basic rules of good navigational practice. Use your eyes to run a commonsense check on position and decide whether or not what you can see ties in with what you ought to see, keep a continuous check on

depth by echo sounder and confirm that it ties in with the charted depth, and record a position on the chart or in the log from time to time so that in the unlikely event of failure of your GPS you have a recent datum position from which to start navigating by other means.

There are several other outputs available on most sets. Their content varies between manufacturers and between models. Most of them come into the 'nice to have' rather than the 'absolutely essential' category. The

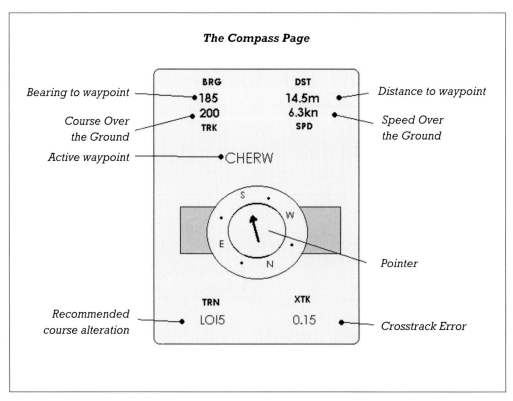

Fig 4.8 The Compass Screen version of the last Highway Screen.

handbooks which come with each set are a good guide to these extra facilities. Do explore them. Even if they are not essential they can often add much to the fun and general interest of navigation.

5 Waypoint navigation

A waypoint is a position, entered by the user and stored in the GPS set's memory. In some user handbooks they are referred to as landmarks. Typically a set will store up to 500 waypoints, each with a six-letter name and usually with a reference symbol such as an anchor, petrol pump or fish to define the type of waypoint. A number of waypoints can be linked to form a route. Every waypoint simply sits in the memory bank until it is made the active or go to waypoint and it then becomes the reference point for navigation.

The use of waypoints is at the heart of GPS navigation. It allows you to navigate with reference to your destination, and to have continuous access to its range and bearing. It is this facility which makes GPS invaluable to the short-handed cruising boat because the skipper or navigator does not have to spend long periods at the chart table while at sea in order to keep the boat safe. Most of the chart table work can be done at the planning stage, before putting to sea.

This doesn't mean that the GPS can do the job of the human navigator – the fact that the GPS is producing information on the range and bearing of the destination does not, of course, mean that it is safe to steer directly towards it. More than one yacht has been lost simply because the navigator steered directly towards a waypoint without bothering to check that there were no rocks or shoals in the way.

ENTERING WAYPOINTS

Most sets offer several different ways of entering waypoints. The simplest is to create a waypoint at the yacht's present position, which is usually just a matter of pressing a single key. This defines the position and you can then add the waypoint name. In cruising yacht navigation the most common reason to enter the present position as a waypoint is for use as the starting point of a route. When racing it is a useful function because it allows you to define the exact position of each mark of a course on the first round. Divers and fishermen are likely to use this function often, to return to the same dive site or fishing mark.

The more usual way to enter a waypoint is as lat. and long.. Almanacs and sailing directions have lists of defined waypoints, which save the trouble of having to take the lat. and long. off the chart. There are, however, a couple of reasons to be wary about using other peoples' waypoint positions. If we all do it we will all try to travel along the same lines, increasing congestion along popular sailing routes. There is also the issue of knowing exactly where the predefined waypoint is: is it exactly in the harbour entrance or a safe distance to seaward of it? If you are using a waypoint's lat. and long. from a published list you will need to plot it on the chart when you come to use it, so you may as well define your own in the first place.

A third option, available on some sets, is to enter a waypoint as a bearing and distance from the present position or from a reference position.

Having defined a waypoint you then need to give it a name and you will usually be restricted to just six letters or numbers. There are no rules about naming waypoints, although it makes them easier to find in an alphabetical list if the first three letters are the same as the first three letters of the nearest significant charted feature. For example, it is better to have waypoints in the east and west entrances to Cherbourg and at Cherbourg marina named as CHERBE, CHERBW and CHERMA rather than ECHERB, WCHERB and MACHER. Apart from that you just have to find abbreviations which make sense to you. You can also give each waypoint a reference symbol if you find it helpful to do so, but this is a facility which I have never found particularly useful.

SELECTING WAYPOINTS

When selecting waypoint positions it is helpful to think about how you are actually going to use them. For instance, when sailing from the Solent to Cherbourg I find it helpful to have a couple of waypoints off Cherbourg harbour, one off the eastern and the other off the western entrance (see Fig 5.1) . The one off the eastern entrance is to seaward

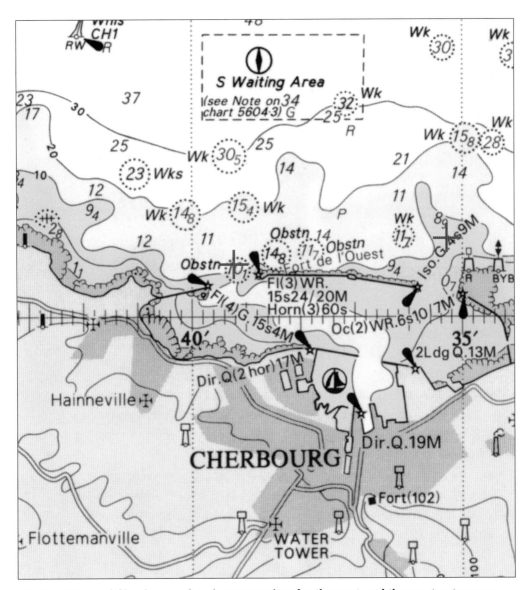

Fig 5.1 Chart of Cherbourg showing waypoints for the east and the west entrances.

of the obstructions on the east side so that it is safe to approach from anywhere to the north.

As a general rule harbour waypoints are easier to use if they are a short distance to seaward of the actual harbour entrance.

When choosing the position for a waypoint which you are going to use as a turning point there is a tendency to be over-generous with the safety margins off the nearest dangers. Try to resist this because if you leave a very wide safety margin at the planning stage you will be tempted to cut the corner when you actually come to use the waypoint and you then enter a grey area 'a bit inshore of the waypoint' - but you don't know exactly how far inside it.

MAN OVERBOARD (MOB)

The Man Overboard function is a special type of waypoint which all sets provide. Many sets have a dedicated Man Overboard key, some have a simple routine of key sequences which have to be followed. The Man Overboard function creates a waypoint at the present position and immediately makes it the active waypoint. The GPS then gives a continuous readout of bearing and distance to the position where the Man Overboard key was pressed. Unfortunately this is not necessarily the same position as the casualty, who will have been carried down tide or current from the position where he went into the water. If all else fails a reasonable tactic for starting a search is to go to the Man Overboard position indicated by GPS and head down tide from there.

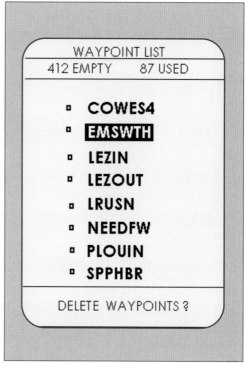

Fig 5.2 Typical waypoint list as displayed on the screen.

The Man Overboard function is a useful one but it is not the total answer to finding the way back to a man overboard on a dark night. Much better not to fall overboard in the first place.

THE WAYPOINT LIST

The GPS receiver will store your waypoints in alphabetical order, but when you scan through the list it will generally only show you the name and reference symbol of each

waypoint (Fig 5.2). If you cannot
remember what your abbreviation for
a particular waypoint means you can
look in detail at an individual waypoint
to find its lat. and long. (Fig 5.3).

You may find it helpful to keep a more
detailed list of your waypoints, in the
order in which you create them, with
the name, abbreviation, lat. and long.
and any relevant comments. The
advantage of keeping the list in
chronological rather than alphabetical
order is that you will often use a group
of waypoints on a particular passage
and these waypoints will naturally
be found in the same part of your list.
In any case alphabetical lists soon
become unmanageable unless you
keep them on an electronic organiser.
A list might be in this form:

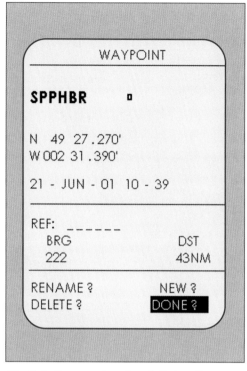

Fig 5.3 Screen showing full details
of a waypoint.

Name	Abbrev.	Lat/Long	Comments
Bembridge Ledge	BEMLED	N 50°40.850' W001°02.050'	l'east of Bembridge Ledge Buoy
Barfleur Harbour	BARHBR	N 49°40.950' W001°13.600'	On leading line. 1.2' ENE of harbour entrance

USING WAYPOINTS

To use a waypoint the convention adopted by most GPS sets is to press the GOTO key, which allows you to select the waypoint you wish to use. The selected waypoint then becomes the active waypoint and the display shows bearing and distance to its position. This is probably the most-used feature of GPS and it is the one which looks as if it lets you navigate without a chart. A typical display in this mode is shown in Fig 5.4.

You also have the option of using the highway display (Fig 5.5) as an indication of direction towards the active waypoint and whether or not you are on track towards it.

The waypoint does not, of course, have to be your destination - as discussed earlier it may be convenient to make the centre

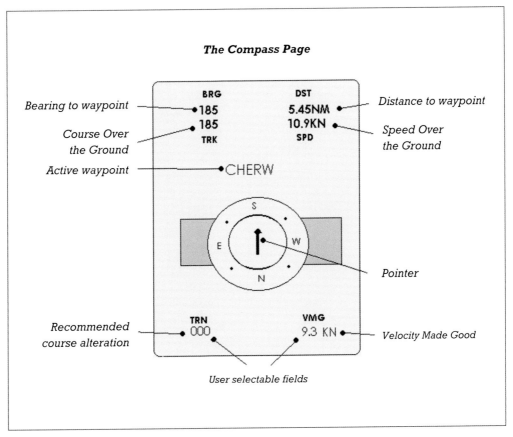

Fig 5.4 Active waypoint information.

of the nearest compass rose the active waypoint, in which case the Highway display will be of no significance.

ROUTES

Routes are formed by linking a number of waypoints. They are extremely useful when you are making a passage which involves rounding a number of headlands or navigational obstructions.

As you build up the Route the display will show the distance and direction for each leg (Fig 5.6). This allows you to check that you haven't inadvertently entered the wrong waypoint or made an error in defining the position of a waypoint.

Most GPS sets limit the number of waypoints in a Route to 30 or so which is more than sufficient for practical navigation. If you find that you need more than 30 waypoints in a Route you

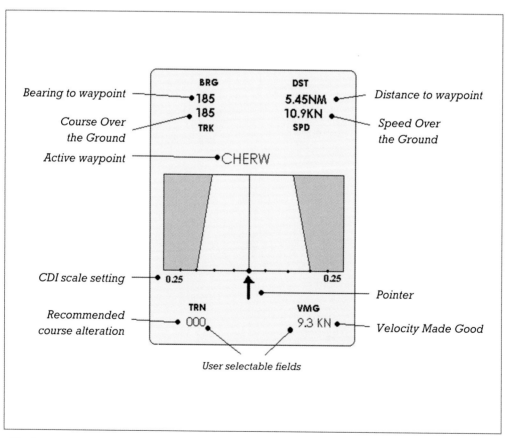

Fig 5.5 The Highway display.

are probably being overcomplicated with your passage planning. There is also a limit to the number of Routes that you can store: 20 or 30 is typical and again this is more than adequate.

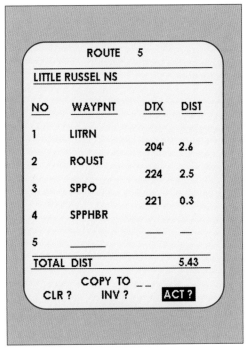

Fig 5.6 Typical display of Route.

6 Passage making

A COASTAL PASSAGE

Let us look at a coastal passage during which, given reasonable visibility, we can expect to remain within sight of land. A good example is the passage from Cherbourg, on the North Coast of France, to St Peter Port in Guernsey.

The total distance from the western entrance to Cherbourg harbour to the entrance to St Peter Port is 42 miles.

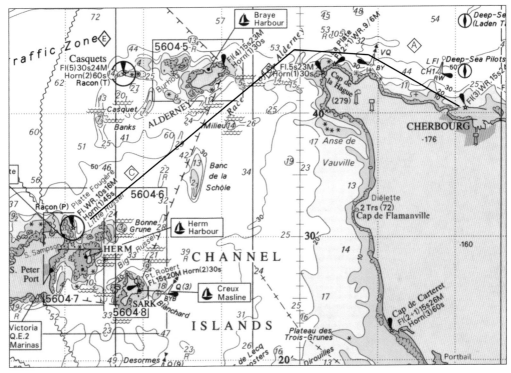

Fig 6.1 Chart extract showing relative positions of Cherbourg and St. Peter Port.

The critical element of this passage for a sailing boat, for which 5 knots is a respectable passage speed, is the tidal streams which run very fast through the Alderney Race, between Cap de la Hague and Alderney, and in the Little Russel, the channel between Guernsey and Herm.

On the day you are to make this passage the morning HW at St Helier is at 0600 UT, 0700 BST which is the time you are working in. The evening HW is at 1820 UT, 1920 BST and it is springs. The tidal diamonds (for positions see Fig 6.1) give you the following information:

TIDAL STREAMS REFERRED TO HW AT SAINT HELIER

Hours		A 49°44'.5N 01°43'.9W	B 49°44'.0N 02°03'.5W	C 49°35'.6N 02°20'.7W
	6	277° 3.4 1.6	220° 5.4 2.5	224° 3.0 1.3
	5	278° 3.3 1.6	216° 5.3 2.5	203° 3.2 1.4
Before	4	280° 2.5 1.2	214° 4.3 2.0	172° 2.3 1.0
High Water	3	279° 1.1 0.5	206° 2.2 1.0	125° 2.4 1.1
	2	282° 0.5 0.2	109° 0.7 0.3	098° 3.4 1.5
	1	083° 2.2 1.0	041° 3.5 1.6	082° 3.3 1.4
High Water	0	090° 3.4 1.6	032° 5.6 2.6	056° 2.5 1.7
	1	098° 3.4 1.6	030° 5.3 2.5	018° 2.4 1.0
	2	112° 2.1 1.0	031° 4.2 2.0	349° 3.0 1.3
After	3	110° 1.3 0.6	033° 2.3 1.0	318° 2.5 1.1
High Water	4	180° 0.2 0.1	114° 0.3 0.1	283° 2.5 1.1
	5	276° 1.5 0.7	221° 2.9 1.2	260° 2.5 1.1
	6	278° 3.0 1.4	221° 5.0 2.4	233° 2.8 1.2

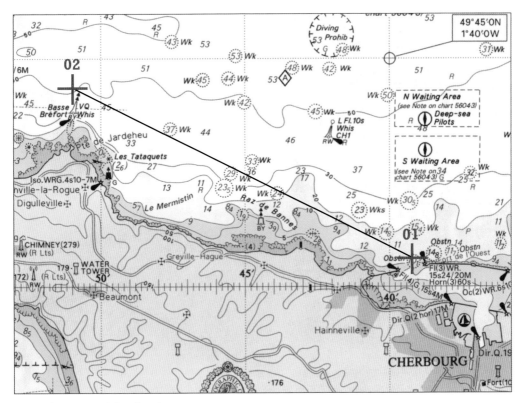

Fig 6.2 Chart of the first leg.

According to this tidal stream information you will have a favourable stream off Cherbourg from about 1130 BST and the stream will be favourable in the Little Russel (the channel between Guernsey and Herm) until 1620 BST. By 1720 the stream will be adverse and flowing at 1.2 knots and by 1920 it will be over 5 knots against, so making your required time of arrival at the Little Russel is essential.

The sailing directions tell you that there is an inshore eddy along the north coast of the Cherbourg peninsular which starts to run to the west 2 hours before the start of the main west-going stream. Hence you could set out from Cherbourg Western Entrance at 0920 and carry a favourable stream for slightly under 7 hours. You will therefore need an average speed over the ground of a little over 6 knots to complete the passage with a favourable stream. Looking at the tidal streams in detail, this should be achievable with a speed through the water of 4 knots.

The departure waypoint we have chosen is 2.5 miles from the marina so we need

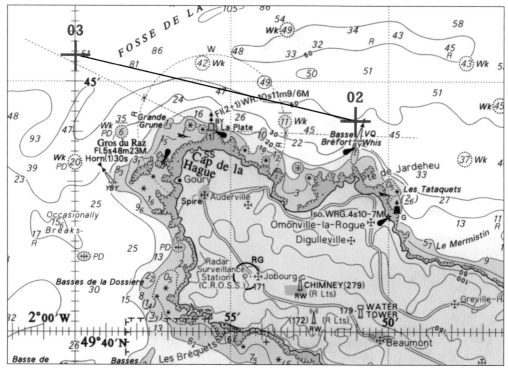

Fig 6.3 Chart of Basse Brefort to Cap de la Hague.

to plan to sail no later than 0845 BST.

The only tidal height restriction on
this passage is the depth of water
over the sill of the inner harbour at
St Peter Port, but there are plenty of
visitors' berths in the outer harbour
which are fine as long as there is not
a strong easterly blowing. The forecast
is for light southwesterlies so there is
no need to worry about tidal heights.

Next we need to look at the route.
The first leg (Fig 6.2) could be direct
from Cherbourg Western Entrance
to Basse Brefort Buoy but you need

to stay as close inshore as possible
until about 1130 to get the maximum
benefit from the inshore eddy and
by the time you arrive at Basse Brefort
the stream will be setting quite hard
to the west so it would be wise to plan
to give it a reasonable berth.

There are two ways you could plan
this leg. You could divide it into
three, Western Entrance to off Raz de
Bannes, thence inshore to a waypoint
off Omonville La Rogue and finally
to a waypoint off Basse Brefort.
Alternatively you could treat it as a
single leg from the Western Entrance

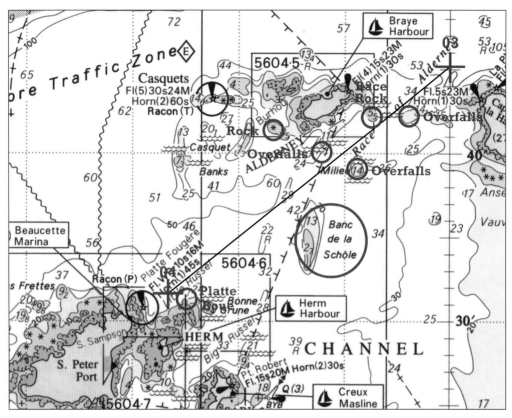

Fig 6.4 Chart of the third leg.

direct to a waypoint 1 mile north of Basse Brefort buoy, planning to tuck in towards the coast after clearing Raz de Bannes until the west-going stream sets in. The second plan has the great merit of simplicity and a generally more flexible approach.

The next section takes you round Cap de la Hague and into the Alderney Race (Fig 6.3) . If all goes according to plan you should be at the northern end of the Race at about 1230 by which time the tidal stream will be setting hard to the southwest. The fast tidal stream flowing over the rocky ledges off Cap de la Hague will throw up a very lumpy sea so we need to give this corner a wide berth. If you aim to pass 1 mile north of La Plate light and continue on the same track to a waypoint on the 2° W meridian, that should do the trick.

From the northern end of the Alderney Race you have a clear run to the northern end of the Little Russel where the final open sea waypoint should be established in a position that is safe to approach from anywhere between a little west of north and a little south of east (Fig 6.4). The reason for pushing this waypoint so far into clear water is that if the wind blows as forecast from the SW you will be beating up to it so you need a clear 90° approach sector. There is no point in trying to work out the tactics for this leg until you know the actual wind direction and strength.

Assuming that pilotage through the Little Russel will be carried out visually all that you need now is a final waypoint in or close to the entrance to St Peter Port harbour so that when you construct the route you will get an accurate distance right to the end of it.

Next we need to list the actual waypoints, which we can do in our waypoint log (see below).

At this stage of the planning it would also be worth having a couple of extra waypoints, for harbours which might be used as diversions during the trip. Suitable ones might be on the leading line 1 mile off Alderney harbour entrance and off Dielette, on the west side of the Cherbourg peninsula. You

Waypoint Log

Name	Abbrev	Lat/Long	Comments
Cherbourg West	CHERW	N 49°40'.200 W001°39'.350	Centre of entrance
Basse Brefort Buoy	BBREBY	N 49°44'.570 W001°51'.050	1' N of Buoy
Cap de la Hague	CAPHAG	N 49°45'.450 W002°00'.000	NE end of Alderney Race
Little Russell North	LRUSN	N 49°31'.800 W002°27'.000	Clear north of N end of Little Russell
St Peter Port Harbour	SPPHBR	N 49°27'.450 W002°30'.750	0.4' off entrance to harbour

also need to read what the Sailing Directions have to say about these harbours and make a note that Alderney is exposed to winds and swell between north and east and Dielette is totally inaccessible at low water springs and dangerous to approach at any state of the tide in strong westerlies.

It might also be helpful to enter a waypoint for the nearest compass rose to the route to make fixing simpler.

The next job is to enter our five waypoints in the GPS and combine them into a route. This will automatically give the bearing and distance for each leg and the route screen on the GPS will look like this:

No	WAYPOINT	BRG	DST
01	CHERW		
		304°	8.7'
02	BBREBY		
		282°	5.9'
03	CAPHAG		
		237°	22'
04	LRUSN		
		214°	5.0'
05	SPPHBR		
TOTAL DST			41.6'

Having entered the route you can now draw the tracks on the charts to make sure that you are not passing too close to any dangers and check that the bearings and distances on the chart agree with the bearings and distances given by the GPS.

You can now transpose the route to your notebook and add whatever notes or comments you might find helpful (see over).

The 'Arrive by' column is an indication of the time at which you should reach each waypoint to be on schedule to make your ETA at the destination. You could go into considerable detail in working out these times, taking into account the tidal stream that you will experience over the rest of the trip. All that I have done in this case is to use the overall required speed of 6 knots throughout. The purpose of the column is to give me warning if I am starting to fall behind schedule. While at sea you will generally be monitoring progress on either the Highway or Compass navigation screen, which will give you an ETA at the next waypoint and you can keep a check on progress without having to switch to the Active Route screen to check on ETA or ETE at destination.

On leg 03, from Cap de la Hague to the Little Russel, you couldn't actually hit Race Rock which has a charted depth of 5.5 m. But the reference to it is included in the notes because with a spring tide running it is likely to create heavy overfalls around it, which would be better avoided. You could enter its position as a waypoint, so that as you approach it you can use the Compass screen of the GPS to make sure that you are not closing it on a steady bearing. For similar reasons you will need to avoid the shallowest part of Banc de la Schole, although it is in much slacker streams than Race Rock and is easier to avoid by simply navigating around it.

You may also find it useful to note, either on the chart or in your notebook, the distances of dangers that you are planning to pass. For leg one,

No	WAYPOINT	BRG	DST	ARR BY	NOTES
01	CHERW			0920	
		304°	8.7′		Favourable eddy inshore. Dangers close to port until clear of Raz de Bannes
02	BBREBY			1050	
		282°	5.9′		Building west going tidal stream, probably setting to port towards end of leg
03	CAPHAG			1150	
		237°	22′		Fast favourable stream. Pass Race Rock 0.75′ to stbd. Probably a windward leg.
04	LRUSN			1530	
		214°	5.0′		Through Little Russell. Visual Pilotage. GPS track not safe to navigate, included for distance only.
05	SPPHBR			1620	
TOTAL DIST			41.7′		

drawn to scale, it might look like
the diagram below.

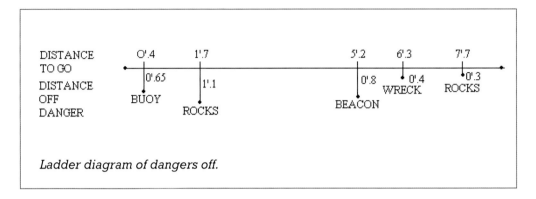

Ladder diagram of dangers off.

Scale drawings can take up a great
deal of unnecessary space and a
simple table is often a more practical
way to store the information.

DANGERS TO PORT		DISTANCE TO GO	DANGERS TO STBD
ROCKY LEDGE	0'.3	7'.7	
DANGEROUS WRECK	0'.4	6'.3	
N CARDINAL BEACON	0'.8	5'.2	
LES TATAQUETS ROCKS	1'.1	1'.7	
BASSE BREFORT BUOY	0'.65	0'.4	

For the third leg (see Fig. 6.4, page 67) the table could be:

DANGERS TO PORT		DTG	DANGERS TO STBD
CHARTED OVERFALLS	0'.9	18'.8	
		16'.4	0'.75 RACE ROCK OVERFALLS
		11' - 15'	1' ALDERNEY S BANKS OVERFALLS
MILIEU OVERFALLS	1'.6	13'.5	
		10'.8	3'.7 PIERRE AU VRAIC ROCK
BANC DE LA SCHOLE	3'	8' - 9'	
PLATTE BOUE	1'.2	0'.7	

Now we will have a look at how you might actually navigate this route, in our hypothetical forecast of light SW winds.

As you clear Cherbourg harbour there are two items of particular interest to you. Can you lay the course to the Basse Brefort waypoint and is your speed made good fast enough to keep you on schedule? There is unlikely to be much cross tide on the first part of this leg so the steering compass will tell you the answer to the first question. You can get confirmation from GPS by looking at the Compass or Highway navigation screen, which will show you the bearing and distance to the first waypoint and your Course Over the Ground. There should be reasonably close agreement between the two. With the wind from the forecast direction this leg should be a close reach.

On the question of speed, you are hoping to pick up the favourable inshore eddy. The simplest way to tell whether or not you have done so is to keep an eye on the fishing floats which seem to abound all around the French coast. The wake on them is the best possible indicator of the direction and strength of the tidal stream. If you are out of luck with fishing floats a comparison between the speed by log and the Speed Over the Ground indicated on the GPS will show whether or not the stream is favourable, but unless you have a particularly accurate log this will not be as accurate as the 'by eye' method.

At this early stage of the passage you may think that Speed Over the Ground is not critical. You may reckon that the tidal streams will be strong and favourable later in the passage so you do not have to worry too much if the GPS Route screen is showing a total passage time of rather more than you need to carry the favourable tide all the way. This would be a mistake. At least half of the passage will probably be to windward so even with strong favourable streams to come you need to keep up a speed over the ground of at least 5 knots. If the wind is not strong enough you may need some assistance from the engine.

Once you are settled on course, and happy that the speed is fast enough, a position fix would be a good idea to confirm that all is well. A lat. and long. plotted on the chart will show which side of the planned track you are and you can compare this with the Crosstrack Error shown on GPS. If the two do not agree you need to check that you haven't made an error in plotting or entering a waypoint.

The first hour of this leg should be low stress from the navigational point of view. If you seem to be encountering a foul stream, as indicated by the fishing floats or the speed over the ground, you need to close the coast. You can use the Highway screen and Crosstrack Error in conjunction with your table of distances off dangers, backed up by a visual check on Raz de Bannes beacon and an eye on the echo sounder, to confirm that you are not getting into dangerously shallow water.

From 1030 onwards you need to keep an eye on the Compass or Highway screen, comparing bearing of the Basse Brefort waypoint with the Course Over the Ground and watching the Crosstrack Error. The tidal stream will soon start to strengthen, running west, and you do not want to be set too far inshore. You also need to keep a good visual lookout for the buoy itself.

You should pass the Basse Brefort waypoint shortly before 1100.

The next leg takes you into a rapidly increasing tidal stream which will be setting quite strongly to port as the leg progresses. Again, the compass or highway screens are going to be the most useful ones to watch. By keeping an eye on Course Over the Ground you get an immediate indication of how hard you are being set off track and how large an alteration of course you need to regain track. If you are concerned that you may be set dangerously far off track, the Highway screen (giving a visual representation of Crosstrack Error) is the one you need to watch, checking the Crosstrack Error against your table of Distances off Danger to see that you have a good safety margin. A fix plotted on the chart, either as lat. and long., or as a bearing and distance from the centre of the compass rose, would be a useful check in the middle of this leg.

It is also very important to navigate by eye on this leg because what you want to avoid is the overfalls and confused seas that form off Cap de la Hague as the southwest going stream starts to gather speed. Exactly how far offshore these will extend is difficult to forecast so you need to keep a close eye out to see if you should give this corner an even wider berth than you planned or if you can safely cut the corner slightly.

As you approach the Cap de la Hague waypoint you need to decide whether or not you will be able to lay the next course of 237° (M) and if not whether you will need to tack or just harden onto the wind, or indeed whether it is going to make more sense to motor directly to windward. For the first half hour of the leg you will be in the fastest part of the Alderney Race and even with quite light winds against a spring ebb tide the sea can be very confused. Unless there is a good firm breeze it could be a good move to roll up the genoa and put the engine on for an hour.

Once past the Cap de La Hague waypoint and into the Race, Speed Over the Ground should increase rapidly and the Navigation screens will give a very optimistic indication of ETA at the next waypoint. You may, at the moment, be making a speed over the ground of something in excess of 10 knots and the GPS will assume that you are going to maintain that speed all the way to your destination. In fact, of course, you will not; the tidal stream will slacken and Speed Over the Ground will drop considerably. At this stage of the passage you need to do manual speed /time/distance sums, using the likely future ground speed, to confirm that you are not going to miss the tide in the Little Russel.

Also at this stage of the passage you need to check that you are passing well clear of Race Rock. If you have it as a waypoint you can quickly check that your course over the ground is not the same as its bearing. Otherwise you need to use the Crosstrack Error to check that you are not more than half a mile to starboard of the planned track and keep a good lookout in the general vicinity of the rock for the profusion of white water that accompanies heavy overfalls. Fixes will be difficult to plot in the violent motion of the Race so checks which don't involve chartwork will be particularly useful and it is in areas such as this that GPS gives the navigator much more confidence than he ever had with visual navigation.

As you emerge from the SW end of the race, with some 12 miles to go to the north end of the Little Russel, you need to decide whether or not you can dispense with the engine, and sail. By now it will be a little after 1300 and the first thing to look at is the speed you need to make good. The GPS Compass or Highway screen will give you distance to go and ETA at the next waypoint, assuming that you maintain the present speed over the ground. Again, your own speed/time/distance

calculation, taking account of predicted tidal stream changes, is going to give a better answer but the GPS will work out the ETE using VMG rather than just speed over the ground.

If you do sail, you need to decide which will be the better tack. There are plenty of variables you need to look at. The first move should be to draw the direct downwind line from the waypoint on the chart and unless there is some overriding factor go for the tack that takes you towards the downwind line. An overriding factor might be a more favourable tidal stream on the other side of the beat or a firm indication that the wind is going to shift. Are there boats to windward of you heading in the same direction? Do they seem to be being lifted or headed?

Once you reach the Little Russel waypoint you should be onto visual pilotage. During the final stages of the approach the accurate positional information which GPS gives you can be a great help in identifying key navigational marks. If you are having difficulty finding a mark take a fix, put on an EP for a few minutes ahead, and measure the bearing of the mark from the EP position. Then look along that bearing, find something (even a distinctive cloud will do) and use it as a reference point for a closer look through binoculars. Your missing mark should then appear.

On a passage such as this the GPS is going to be a very useful aid to navigation and it may seem that you need do nothing more than plan the route and navigate on the Highway screen all the way. This would be dangerous because you would have no defence against simple errors such as misreading a digit on the screen. Some of the information you need, such as the precise extent of the overfalls off Cap de la Hague, just isn't on the chart and the only way you will judge this corner to best advantage is by using your eyes intelligently. And do please remember those expensive warship groundings; you can avoid joining them by carrying out some very simple checks such as plotting the occasional fix which is independent of waypoints, comparing the charted depth with depth by echo sounder and using your eyes to confirm that the land, the buoys and the beacons are all where you expect them to be.

Now here is what the coastal passage looks like in real life....

1. The departure point, the western entrance to Cherbourg.

2. *Cap de la Hague looking south, with a strong south-going stream.*

3. Approaching Cap de la Hague at sea level.

4. Approaching the Alderney Race.

5. In the Alderney Race.

6. The wake of the beacon shows that the tides run strongly in the Little Russel.

7. *The Little Russel from the air.*

8. Journey's end – the outer harbour at St Peter Port.

AN OFFSHORE PASSAGE

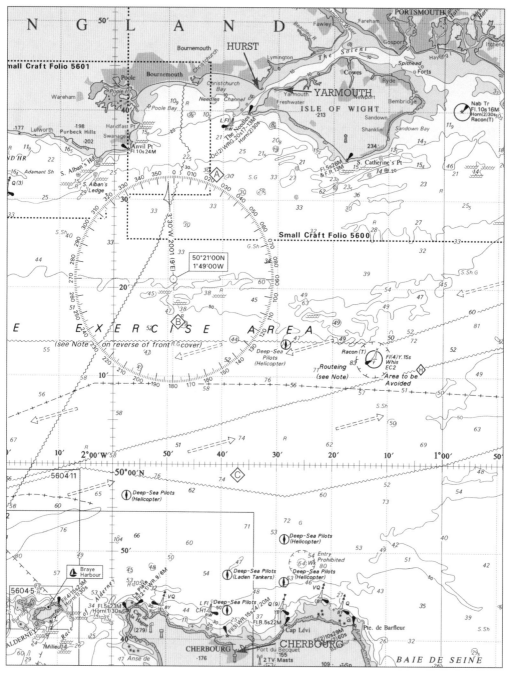

Fig 6.5.

As an example of an offshore passage let us look at the trip from Yarmouth Isle of Wight to Cherbourg, again in a sailing yacht and assuming a 5 knot passage speed (Fig 6.5). This time the only tidal stream restriction is in Hurst Narrows where the streams run at up to 5 knots at springs, so there is no point in trying to pass through against the tide.

The total distance from Yarmouth to Cherbourg is 66 miles of which the first six are down the Needles Channel so the open water crossing is 60 miles.

High Water Dover is at 0040 UT, 0140 BST and again at 1300 UT, 1400 BST. The tidal streams through Hurst Narrows are west going from HW Dover -1 to HW Dover +5, east going from HW Dover +5 to HW Dover -1.

The tidal streams at the three relevant tidal diamonds in the Channel are:

Hours		A 50°33'.0N 01°36'.3W			B 50°16'.0N 01°48'.0W			C 49°59'.0N 01°37'.0W		
	6	090°	0.7	0.3	072°	0.8	0.4	061°	0.8	0.4
	5	092°	2.2	1.1	080°	2.4	1.2	081°	2.6	1.3
Before	4	094°	3.4	1.7	084°	3.5	1.7	085°	4.1	2.1
High Water	3	096°	3.5	1.7	086°	3.5	1.7	084°	4.2	2.1
	2	096°	2.4	1.2	088°	2.5	1.3	086°	3.3	1.7
	1	100°	0.9	0.4	099°	1.2	0.6	084°	1.6	0.8
High Water	2	258⁰	1.1	0.5	238°	0.7	0.4	287°	0.4	0.2
	1	268°	2.1	1.1	263°	2.3	1.1	268°	2.4	1.2
	2	271°	3.4	1.7	270°	3.4	1.7	263°	3.7	1.9
After	3	272°	3.1	1.5	266°	3.3	1.6	258°	4.2	2.1
High Water	4	269°	2.4	1.2	265°	2.6	1.3	259°	3.4	1.7
	5	267°	1.1	0.5	265°	1.5	0.7	266°	2.2	1.1
	6	070°	0.7	0.3	040°	0.2	0.1	332°	0.4	0.2

In order to carry a fair tide through Hurst Narrows and down to the Needles you are going to have to have to leave Yarmouth before about 0515 or after 1300. The early morning start is very early but should give you a daylight passage, whereas the lunchtime start will probably mean an arrival time at Cherbourg of about 0200. Let us go for the early morning start.

There are probably only three waypoints needed for the route for this passage, plus one for the other entrance to Cherbourg harbour in case it becomes more appropriate to use and one for a mid-channel compass rose, see below.

The route to enter in the GPS will be:

No	WAYPOINT	BRG	DST
01	YARHBR		
		239°	5.4'
02	NEEDLE		
		183°	59.0'
03	CHERE		
TOTAL DIST			64.4'

The first leg is, of course, meaningless, because the direct route from Yarmouth to the SW end of the Needles Fairway is over land.

Name	Abbrev	Lat/Long	Comments
Yarmouth Harbour	YARHBR	N 50°42'.650 W001°30'.000	Yarmouth Harbour entrance
Needles	NEEDLE	N 50°39'.500 W001°37'.300	SW end of Needles Fairway (Bridge buoy)
Cherbourg E Entrance	CHERE	N 49°41'.050 W001°35'.450	Close N of entrance
Cherbourg W Entrance	CHERW	N 49°40'.200 W001°39'.350	Centre of entrance
Compass Rose 2	CR2	N 50°21'.000 W001°49'.000	English Channel Central

Transferring the route to your notebook you might annotate it as:

No	WAYPOINT	BRG	DST	NOTES
01	YARHBR			
		239°	5.4'	Not a navigable leg. Do not try to sail.
02	NEEDLE			
		183°	59.0'	Cross Channel. Alternative waypoint at Cherbourg
03	CHERE			W available if needed.
		TOTAL DIST	64.4'	

This is such a simple route that there is a temptation not to bother about it, simply set off from the Needles and enter Cherbourg East as the active waypoint. This would be perfectly acceptable as long as you did not want to have access to a Crosstrack Error reading during the long leg across the channel but this could be useful so the route is worth entering.

The next stage in the plan is to decide what course to steer on departure from the Needles Channel. To do this you need to have some sort of estimate of probable speed. The forecast is for a moderate westerly wind so a speed of 5 knots would certainly be reasonable. It would be sensible to allow a little time in hand to clear the Needles Channel with some west-going stream to run so you plan to be at the departure point at 0610. The tidal streams you are likely to experience during the crossing are:

Ref	+/- HW	TIMES BETWEEN	DRN WEST	DIST GOING	DRN EAST	DST GOING
A	+5	0610-0710	267°	1.1'		
A	+6	0710-0730			070°	0.2'
A	-6	0730-0830			090°	0.7'
A	-5	0830-0930			092°	2.2'
A	-4	0930-1030`			094°	3.4'
B	-3	1030-1130			086°	3.5'
B	-2	1130-1230			088°	2.5'
B	-1	1230-1330			099°	1.2'
B	HW	1330-1430	238°	0.7'		
C	+1	1430-1530	268°	2.4'		
C	+2	1530-1630	263°	3.7'		
C	+3	1630-1730	258°	4.2'		
C	+4	1730-1810	259°	2.3'		
Total streams:			**West-going 14.4'**		**East-going 13.7'**	

The stream east – stream west balance is not the most accurate way of working out tidal stream effects during a 12 hour passage, because the streams do not run due east and west and neither do they run exactly across the track. To do a really accurate job you would have to draw out the set for each hour and you could then find exactly what the resultant would be. However there are several larger approximations, such as the speed at which you will sail, the accuracy with which the helmsman will steer the course and the amount of leeway, all of which would be difficult to quantify with any great degree of accuracy. The "stream east - stream west" balance is therefore a very practical way to predict the overall effect of tidal stream and hence the course to steer for this sort of passage.

With a balance of tidal stream of just 0.7' over a 12 hour passage you can safely ignore it and set out direct for your destination. It would be somewhat over-fastidious to ask the helmsmen to steer 183° for 12 hours. 185° would be a much more realistic course to ask for because it gives the helmsman an actual mark on the compass card to aim for and leaves a little in hand for leeway. When GPS gives you very precise figures there is a temptation to feel

that you have to use them. You don't, it is more important to be practical and use your common sense.

There is also a temptation to use the Crosstrack Error to keep the yacht on the direct line from point of departure to destination. This would not be a good idea. On this passage you would have to steer 225° (M) to remain on track between 1030 and 1130 and your speed over the ground would be down to $3^1/_2$ knots. Later, between 1630 and 1730 you would have to steer 125° (M) to remain on track and again your ground speed would be down to $3^1/_2$ knots. So in those two hours alone you would have lost 30% of your potential speed.

You do, of course, have to check that by steering the same course all the way and allowing the boat to be carried well off the direct track you are not allowing her to be carried into danger. If you want to do this in detail you can add an extra column to the tidal stream predictions to show how far east or west of track you will be throughout the leg (see page 94).

Plotting this on the chart (Fig 6.6) you can see that you will pas very close to Le Pierre Noire north cardinal buoy, to the north of Cap Levi . This is something you are going to have

Ref	+/- HW	TIMES BETWEEN	DRN	DIST	DRN	DST	TOTAL WEST	TOTAL EAST
A	+5	0610-0710	267°	1.1'			1.1	
A	+6	0710-0730			070°	0.2'	0.9'	
A	-6	0730-0830			090°	0.7'	0.2'	
A	-5	0830-0930			092°	2.2'		2.0'
A	-4	0930-1030`			094°	3.4'		5.4'
B	-3	1030-1130			086°	3.5'		8.9'
B	-2	1130-1230			088°	2.5'		11.4'
B	-1	1230-1330			099°	1.2'		12.6'
B	HW	1330-1430	238°	0.7'				11.9'
C	+1	1430-1530	268°	2.4'				9.5'
C	+2	1530-1630	263°	3.7'				5.8'
C	+3	1630-1730	258°	4.2'				1.6'
C	+4	1730-1810	259°	2.3'			0.7'	

to keep a careful eye on as you approach the French coast.

Looking at the probable ground track for a passage is not something I would expect to do in such detail for every passage. A brief look at the tidal sets will usually be enough to identify areas in which you might need to take a closer look and even modify the original plan.

Now for the actual navigation during the channel crossing. You have not done any detailed planning to use the GPS on the way out of the Solent and down the Needles Fairway, so the navigation, as opposed to pilotage, really starts as you get out into the open sea.

Once you have settled down on course you will know very quickly whether or not your planned speed is accurate and therefore whether or not you need to modify your Course To Steer. A useful rule of thumb for approximating Course To Steer is

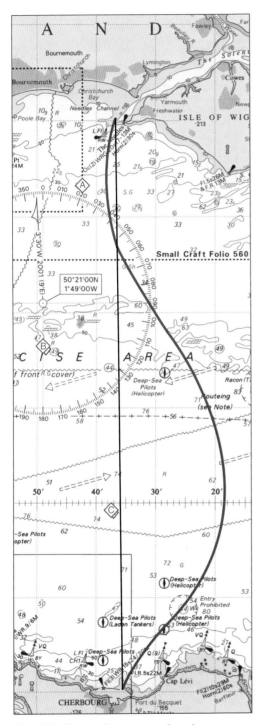

*Fig 6.6 Chart of passage showing
the actual ground track followed.*

that on a 60 mile passage each mile
of unbalanced tidal set requires
a 1° course alteration to counteract
it. You can play around with simple
proportion - on a 15 mile passage
a 1 mile tidal set requires a 4° course
alteration, and as long as you are
not looking at course alterations
of more than about 15° it is
reasonably accurate.

If, for instance, you found that you
were actually sailing at 6 knots
instead of the predicted 5 you would
take only 10 hours instead of 12 to
complete the leg. This means that
the total westward tidal set would
be reduced by 7.7' to 6.7' and the
balance of tidal set for the passage
would now be 7' east instead of 0.7'
west. You would need a new course
to steer of 190° (M) or 195° (M) if
you want to allow for a little leeway.

Having worked out the actual Course
To Steer, a GPS fix by lat. and long.
or bearing and distance from the
compass rose would be useful.
The aim is to check that the charted
direction and distance from the fix to
your destination ties in with bearing
and distance to next waypoint given
by the GPS. It would also be sensible
to note the depth by echo sounder
at the time of the fix and compare
it with the charted depth, corrected
for height of tide. Early on in the

passage it gives confidence to confirm that all the navigational systems are functioning correctly.

You can now set up the navigational routine for the passage. With the GPS set to the Compass or Highway screen you have a continuous output of bearing and distance to your destination, Course and Speed Over the Ground and ETA. The Course and Speed Over the Ground will vary from hour to hour as the tidal rates change. You can also use the Highway page and Crosstrack Error to confirm that the tidal stream is carrying you away from or back towards the track by the amounts you would expect.

It is good practice to plot a fix on the chart every hour, noting the time and log reading in the log. Then if disaster strikes and the GPS ceases to function you have up-to-date information on which to base visual and dead reckoning navigation.

As well as monitoring progress you have to make decisions about whether or not the course you are steering needs adjustment. You don't need to do this too often - a reasonable rule of thumb is to recalculate every time you halve the distance left to run or if the speed changes by more than a knot.

By applying the check every time the distance halves you will be looking at the Course To Steer with ever-increasing frequency as you approach your destination, which makes sense. You don't want to be fiddling around with small alterations every hour when you still have 50 miles to go but you have to get it exactly right at the end of the passage.

You also need to keep an eye on any forecast changes in the weather and the way that they might affect your speed, or even cause you to question whether Cherbourg is still a sensible destination.

During the final hour of the passage the two most helpful GPS outputs are the Bearing of the Waypoint and the Course Over the Ground. The tidal stream probably isn't going to change much over an hour so you want to steer a course which will match the Bearing to Destination with Course Over the Ground. As soon as you can see enough detail on the land to pick yourself a clear transit you can concentrate more on that than on the GPS screen.

GPS certainly takes most of the

(Right) Spot on with GPS: The turning mark in this race is the Fastnet Rock, reached after sailing across the Irish Sea.

navigational worry out of passages out of sight of land. No longer is poor visibility a real threat from the navigational point of view. It is, of course, important to remember that GPS does nothing to improve the lookout you can keep for approaching ships, and a collision in deep water is more likely to be fatal than a grounding from which you might well be able to walk ashore. The go/no-go decisions taken in poor visibility must generally take more account of likely traffic density and whether or not you have radar, than navigational hazards and your ability to navigate around them.

OCEAN PASSAGES

With traditional navigational methods the further offshore one ventured the less accurate became the methods of fixing position. With GPS that has all changed - you can now know exactly where you are all the time. With a sextant as the primary navigational instrument the navigator was more than happy if he could obtain a position at morning and evening twilight, with a running fix at noon and possibly in mid-afternoon. With GPS the only limit on the number of times a day he can plot a position is the distance he has to sail in order to have moved

far enough across a very small scale chart to have room to plot another fix on it.

The most frequently asked question about ocean navigation with GPS is "Should I take and learn to use a sextant in case of GPS failure?" The practical answer is that a hand-held GPS, with its own batteries and plenty of spares is likely to be a more practical backup. If you are worried about a GPS system failure, or a switch off by the US Department of Defense in a time of heightened political or diplomatic tension, then you must buy yourself a sextant, some nautical tables and learn how to use them. Since nearly all the world's ocean crossings are made in an east-west direction a knowledge of how to take and work out a noon latitude sight should be sufficient for emergency use, then you can get yourself onto the latitude of your destination and run down the Easting or Westing - you will certainly arrive at the right place but when you will arrive will be a bit of a mystery until it happens.

One great bonus of GPS sets is that the distance and direction of one waypoint from another or of a waypoint from the present position which they give is actually

the great circle, the shortest distance. At distances of under a few hundred miles there is no practical difference between a rhumb line (a straight line on a Mercator chart) and a great circle but on an ocean crossing the rhumb line distance may be hundreds of miles longer than the great circle. The computer in a GPS gives an instant great circle bearing of the destination from the present position, a calculation which, just a few years ago, involved much toil with nautical tables or spherical trigonometry. Suffice to say that for navigation on an ocean passage, GPS is The Business.

RECORD KEEPING

There are several reasons for
keeping a navigational log.
In the unlikely event of a total
failure of the GPS receiver it is
important to have sufficient records
to start navigating by visual
methods or by dead reckoning.
A record of the weather, particularly
wind direction and strength and
barometric pressure are extremely
useful aids to keeping track of
a developing weather situation
and help you to build up a more
detailed forecast of the local
weather than you can hope to get

TIME	CRSE T/M/C	LOG DIST	LAT /LONG OR WPT BRG/DST
0945			
1015		0	
1100	185°	3.7	CHERE 202° 71.6'
1200	185°	8.2	CHERE 203° 67.0'
1220			
1300	185°	13.1	CHERE 202° 61.6'
1400	200°	19.3	CHERE 201° 53.8'
1600	200°	31.5	CHERE 194° 36.4'
1700	200°	36.4	CHERE 193° 31.2'
1800	200°	41.9	CHERE 194° 24.5'
1930			
2000	200°	53.1	CHERE 195° 13.6'
2130	200°	62.8	CHERE 187° 6.1'
2155			

FROM *Chichester Harbour*.....TOWAR

LOGBOOK

FOR GPS NAVIGATION

erbourg.............DATE *12 Jul 02*..TIMEZONE *-1*...GPS DATUM.*WGS 84*....VAR *3°W.*

NARRATIVE	WIND DIR/STR	BAR
ine on. Slipped mooring, motor clear of harbour		
rway Bn abeam to Stbd. Engine off. Set main + genoa. Course 185° M	*WNW 4*	*1012*
	W 3	*1013*
id falling light, on engine, furled genoa.		
ar of Bembridge Ledge, A/C 200°.		
ck fix 50° 37'.72N 01° 02'.36W. Depth by echo sounder 17m.	*Lt Var*	*1013*
	SSE 1	*1012*
5 Wind filling in from SE, set genoa. 1640 Off engine.		
	SSE 4	*1011*
0 Cirrus cloud moving in from W. Wind increasing and backing. 1 reef in main		
	SE 5	*1010*
id continuing to increase. 2nd reef in main + 5 rolls in genoa.		
ibility reduced by drizzle.	*SE 5*	*1009*
0 Visibility < 2'. Sea building.		
ck fix by GPS agrees with bearing and distance to waypoint. CTS 205° M		
erbourg E entrance visible. Wind inreasing. On engine, stowed all sail. Course as		
quired to enter harbour. 2230 Entered Rade de Cherbourg. 2310 Berthed port		
le to in visitor's berth. Engine off.		

Engine Hours c/f *12.5*...**Today** *5.6*......**Total** *18.1*....

from shipping forecasts.

A record of how your boat performs in different conditions is also useful to have and can be built up in more detail from reasonably detailed navigational records than from a general impression of how she sails. You also need to keep a record of engine hours so that you can carry out maintenance routines such as oil changes at the right intervals.

It is generally convenient to use the same workbook for both passage planning and for record keeping. I have designed Fernhurst Books' *LOGBOOK FOR GPS NAVIGATION* (ISBN I 898660 94 8) for both yacht and powerboat navigators.

There is a pair of pages for each trip: first comes a planning page, followed by a log page designed to help you record information during the trip.

Many skippers keep much more detailed records of their cruises, with photographs or drawings of the ports and anchorages visited and sketch plans of the smaller havens for which no detailed chart exists. These can be great fun to compile and some of the less inhibited accounts of the human side of a cruise make hilarious reading. They can be both a useful guide for friends who plan to visit the cruising area described and good reading for long winter evenings. They do, however, need to be kept separate from the navigational log, which becomes less useful if the important information becomes cluttered with superfluous detail.

So much for the theory. Here is the offshore passage for real....

1. The departure point: Yarmouth, Isle of Wight (looking south).

2. The Needles – heading out of the Solent, bound for France.

3. Nearly there.
Get the French
courtesy flag ready.

4. *Cherbourg marina.*

7 Pilotage

Traditionally, pilotage was navigation in narrow channels and around harbours, where considerable accuracy was required and was achieved mainly by the use of leading and clearing lines and transits. GPS certainly has the accuracy to be a useful pilotage aid. There is an obvious psychological barrier to using satellites, thousands of miles away, as the reference points by which to navigate safely between rocks a few boat lengths on either side, but is there any logical reason to mistrust GPS for such close and detailed work?

There are indeed questions about the inherent accuracy of the system which have to be asked before putting total

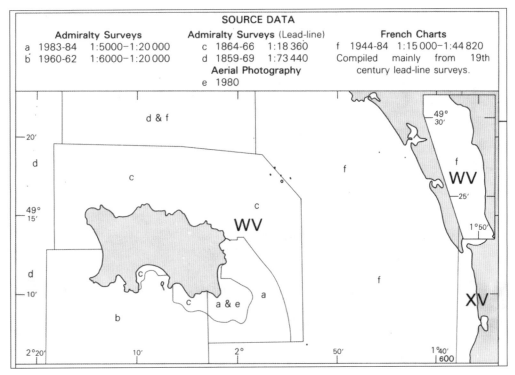

Fig 7.1 Source Data diagram for a chart of Jersey.

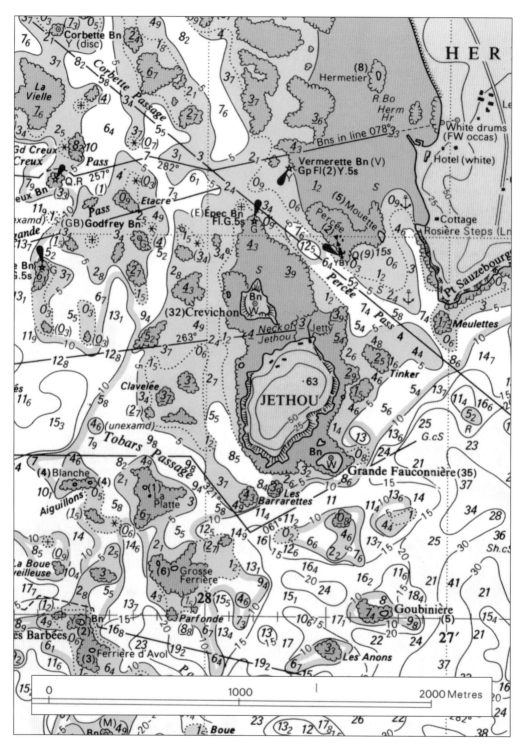

Fig 7.2 The passages south of Herm.

faith in GPS for close pilotage. Can you be certain of the absolute, as opposed to relative, accuracy of the chart? You need to look at the source information from which it was compiled to see how old it is. Most British Admiralty charts include a diagram which shows the dates of the surveys from which the chart was compiled (see Fig 7.1). If it is based on surveys more than 50 years old and you need to be accurate to a few metres, you should certainly be hesitant about using GPS positions, which may have excellent accuracy in absolute terms, rather than seeking the relative accuracy of marks which are close enough to see. Hydrographic surveyors have always been meticulous about accuracy but in the days before electronic position fixing systems they were limited in what they could achieve by the fact that all they had to work with was visual observations of angles and physical measurements of distance. What they managed to achieve was quite astounding, particularly in terms of the relative positions of features, but inevitably the absolute accuracy decayed as they moved away from their datum reference point.

It often comes as a surprise to see the extent to which surveys over 100 years old are still the best reference for areas around the coasts of Europe. As an example, the Source Data Diagram on the 1994 chart of Jersey shows that the most up-to-date detailed information on the north coast comes from lead and line surveys carried out in the middle of the 19th century (Fig 7.1).

As we have already mentioned, you must have total confidence that your GPS is on the same datum as the chart or you could have inherent errors of up to a couple of hundred metres.

How accurate do you really need to be? Some channels demand that you position the boat to within a few metres in order to avoid the hazards and this is perfectly possible using a good visual transit or 'handrailing' (passing as close as possible) round a rock or beacon. A good example is the passages south of Herm in the Channel Islands . As the chart shows (Fig 7.2), there is so little clearance off some of the rocks that there can be no substitute for visual positioning, a 15 m error would have you high and dry.

You also have to bear in mind that pilotage is more than just establishing position, you have to be able to detect a cross current which is setting you off track and compensate for it, quickly and accurately. GPS is good

at this, because it gives a continuous
read-out of Course and Speed Over
the Ground, but figures changing
on a screen do not give as good an
appreciation of rate of sideways set
or the effectiveness of a course
alteration to counteract it as do the
relative movement of the marks in
a good visual transit.

You also have to consider the extent
to which you can pilot the boat
successfully if you are concentrating
on numbers on a screen rather on
the world around you. In many
pilotage situations you will be in
heavy traffic, surrounded by other
boats and ships which you need to
keep an eye on. There will be visual
clues such as the wake on a buoy
ahead which will give you an
indication of the direction and

rate of the tidal stream which you are about to encounter. Gathering clouds on the windward horizon foretell an impending deterioration in the weather. There are a host of other visual clues which you could well miss if you are paying too much attention to data transmitted to you from space and displayed on a screen, rather than to your immediate surroundings.

So much for the negative aspects of GPS. It also has great merit for close pilotage. Do not be put off using it by the generalised warnings about its unsuitability for pilotage which appear in the introduction to many volumes of yachtsmen's sailing directions, most of which were written before Selective Availability was set to zero and when there were random inaccuracies of up to 200 metres in GPS positions.

While the techniques of pilotage, based on clearing and leading lines, have traditionally differed from those of coastal navigation, where the primary techniques were visual position fixing and estimated positions, GPS does not require any such distinction and pilotage using GPS is very similar to coastal navigation, it just has to be carried out to tighter margins of accuracy.

QUICK CLEARING LINES AND LEADING LINES

There are occasions as you close the land when your main interest will be in knowing that you are clear of danger rather than in knowing exactly where you are and GPS can be particularly helpful with this.

Let us take the example of approaching the north end of the Little Russel from the northeast, with the tidal stream setting to the south (Fig 7.3). The danger here is being set onto the off-lying rocks to the north of Herm. Ideally you will be heading directly towards a waypoint in open water, well clear of all dangers and keeping careful track of progress on the chart. There are, however, occasions when things do not go according to plan and our actual navigation falls some way short of the ideal. You have been set to the south of your planned track, the westerly wind is increasing rapidly, the sea building and it is starting to rain. Faces in the cockpit are taking on a greenish tinge. You need a quick and easy-to-execute plan to keep the boat safe in the final approach to the Little Russel.

The most northerly of the dangers north of Herm is Platte Boue at latitude

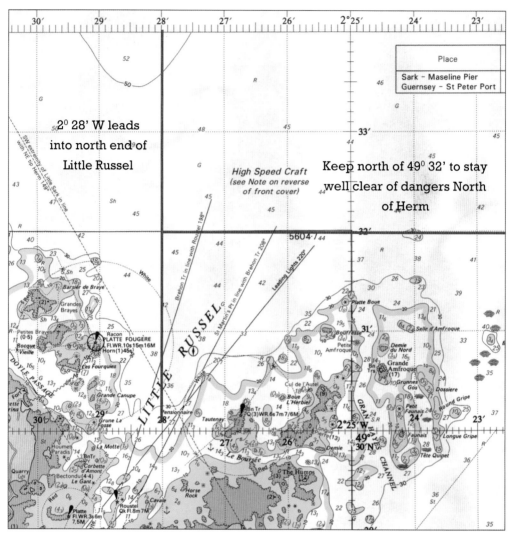

Fig 7.3 Quick leading and clearing lines for the north end of the Little Russel.

49° 31'.3N. If you keep north of 49° 32'N you will be in deep water with a generous margin of safety. Once you reach the line of longitude 2° 28'W you are clear to turn south along it because it leads clear down into the channel with a good margin of safety on each side and brings

you into reasonably sheltered water close enough to Roustel for you to pick up a visual pilotage plan through the narrow part of the channel. You could, if you can spend the time at the chart table, work out a more sophisticated plan which would involve a shorter distance to travel but the great thing about using parallels of latitude and meridians of longitude is that they are very quick to plot, they can keep you safe with the absolute minimum of time spent at the chart table, and the plan is easy to remember.

A PRACTICE TO AVOID

There is a temptation, particularly in a fast powerboat in which chartwork is almost impossible while at sea, to plan pilotage in well buoyed areas like the Solent as a series of legs between buoys. There are a number of reasons why this isn't a good idea, with or without GPS. First and foremost, if you plan to hit a buoy, sooner or later you will succeed and you won't be the first to have scored a direct hit. At night in particular it is quite difficult for the helmsman to judge the distance from a buoy so it is better not to make a habit of pointing him at them.

Secondly, you will probably have a very complex pilotage plan, with many more legs than it needs and small course alterations at every buoy.

The navigation authorities who lay and maintain buoys try to keep the buoy-to-buoy lines in safe water for the ships for whose benefit the channels are marked, so if you follow these lines you will be encroaching on waters where deep draft ships have to navigate, whereas in a shallow draft boat you could plan to be well clear of them.

If everyone used the buoys as waypoints the routes between them would be very crowded places, with two-way traffic charging each other head on.

Buoys have a very useful function in helping you to monitor progress along a leg so they should certainly not be ignored, but they are not generally intended to mark the centre of a navigational channel and it is a mistake to use them as if they were.

PILOTAGE PLANS

Pilotage plans are very often based on advice in Sailing Directions and these are all written on the assumption that visual pilotage techniques will be used. No matter, the recommended visual route will very often be the best one available and if the planned tracks can be followed with reference to visual marks or to GPS you have the ideal situation of two separate systems which you can use to cross check against each other.

Let us look at the approach to St Peter Port, Guernsey, from the north (Fig 7.4),

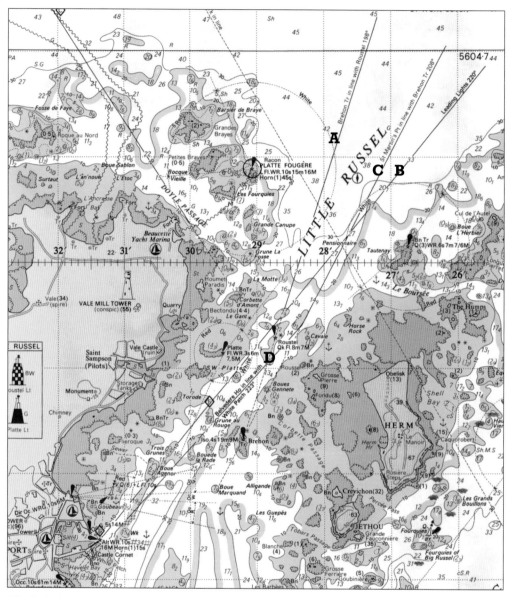

Fig 7.4 Chart extract of Little Russel, showing the recommended leading lines.

through the Little Russel. The chart shows four leading lines:

A Brehon Tower in line with Roustel, 198°(T)

B Leading lights in line, 220°(T)

C St Martin's Point (SE corner of Guernsey) in line with Brehon Tower, 208°(T)

D Belvedere House in line with white patch on Castle Cornet, 223°(T)

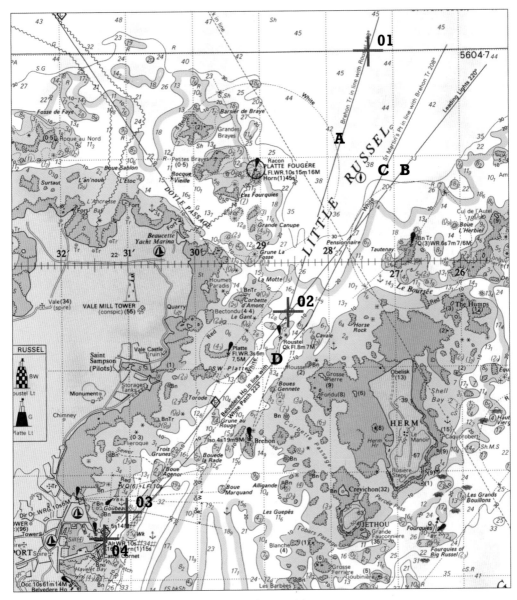

Fig 7.5 Little Russel chart showing waypoint positions.

Line A has the advantage that both marks are easy to identify. You can follow it until close North of Roustel, then turn onto line B, to pass West of Roustel. Both the marks for line C are also easy to identify, although St Martin's Point is some 7 miles away when you want to pick up the line and hence this route requires reasonable visibility. Line C leads

down to line D, which you must pick up to pass East of Roustel, or you could start on line C and transfer onto line B to pass West of Roustel.

It would be possible simply to follow line B all the way through, although the Sailing Directions warn against this. It leads close (0'.5) NW of the drying rock Platte Boue and yachts arriving at St Peter Port from the North are likely to have taken the fair stream down the Alderney Race or the Swinge (the passage west of Alderney), hence arriving near to low water when there is a SE set onto the rocks north of Herm. Another problem with attempting to use this line throughout is that the rear leading mark is decidedly inconspicuous in daylight.

The simplest and safest route is line A to north of Roustel, then line B to the harbour entrance. Adapting this for GPS use the first stage of the planning is to select suitable waypoints. These could be:

No	Abbrev	Name	Lat/Long	Notes
01	LITRN	Little Russel North end	49° 32'.0N 02° 27'.35W	Start of pilotage south through Little Russel, on the leading line Brehon Tr x Roustel 202°(M).
02	ROUST	Roustel	49° 29'.53N 02° 28'.59W	Turning point close N of Roustel onto leading line St Peter Port Leading Lights 224°(M).
03	SPPO	St Peter Port Outer	49° 27'.64N 02° 31'.06W	In clear water, 0'.3 off St Peter Port harbour entrance.
04	SPPHBR	St Peter Port Harbour	49° 27'.37N 02° 31'.39W	Centre of St Peter Port harbour entrance.

These are shown in Fig 7.5 and can now be entered into the GPS and combined into a route, which will give a route screen as shown in Fig 7.6.

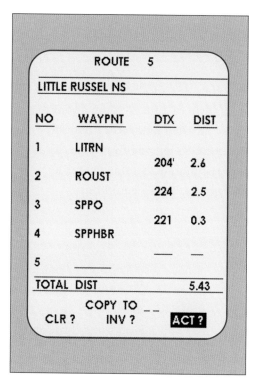

Fig 7.6 Route screen for Little
Russel pilotage.

There is a temptation to do without
waypoint 3 because from the North
it is easy to go direct to the harbour
entrance. However you may well
have to hang around off the harbour
waiting for large ships to leave and it
is useful to have a waypoint close off
the entrance to which you can return
safely from more or less any direction.

We now have a basic route to which
we need to add some information
which will allow us to deviate slightly
from our planned track, which we
may well need to do in order to get
out of the way of other boats or to

miss fishing floats, with which the
area abounds. There are two ways
we could do this. We could work out
clearing bearings from waypoints
2 and 3 for use on the first and second
legs, as shown on the chart (Fig 7.7).
This tells us that on the first leg we
have to keep the bearing to waypoint
reading between 177° and 232° and on
the second leg it must be between
218° and 234°.

The other way to establish where the
safe water lies would be to use the
Crosstrack Error. The chart shows
that there are a number of dangers
on each leg (Fig 7.8) and it would be
possible to compile a table showing
the distance to next waypoint and
distance off track that these dangers
lie. This would, however, result in
a rather complicated tabulation and
it would be much simpler to take
the distance of the nearest danger
to the track and make a note of this,
establishing a corridor in which you
can navigate with complete safety.
This would give:

On leg 1,   Cross Track Error not to
            exceed 0'.3 to Starboard,
            0'.5 to Port.
On leg 2,   0.18 to Starboard,
            0'.3 to Port.
(It seems reasonable to assume that
you don't need to include Roustel
itself in the clearing ranges, you

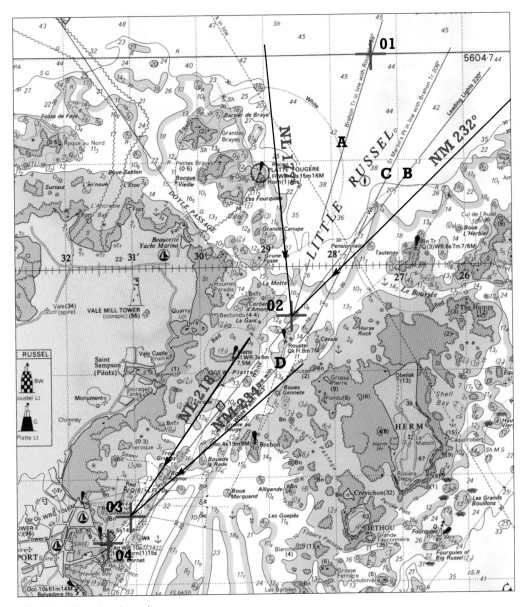

Fig 7.7 Clearing bearings.

simply have to avoid it by eye.)

In a pilotage plan with longer legs it
might well be more sensible to make
a table of distances off dangers, exactly

like the ladder diagram described in
Chapter 6 for coastal passages.

Carrying out any plan which can be
executed by GPS or by visual pilotage

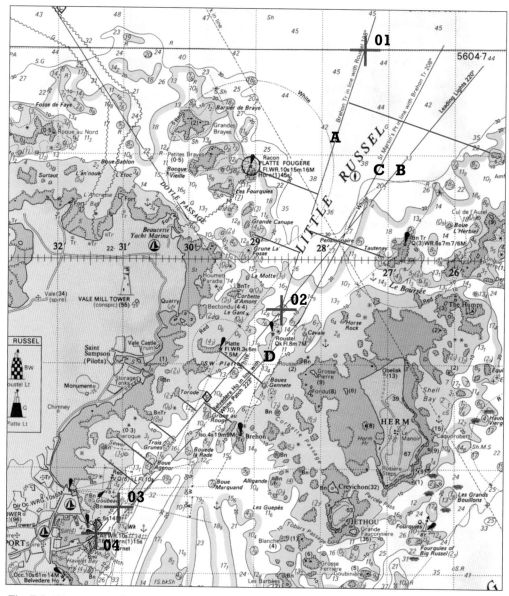

Fig 7.8 Distances off dangers.

it often works out that the GPS is used in the outer approaches, from where the visual marks become progressively easier to identify as the range closes. Visual pilotage then becomes the primary means of navigation, with the GPS being used as confirmation that the boat is on the planned track. This routine works particularly well when entering an unfamiliar harbour or channel for the first time and takes much of the worry out of narrow channels where the leading marks are initially difficult to pick up.

PILOTAGE IN POOR VISIBILITY

Before the days of yacht radar and accurate electronic navaids the lack of position finding capability was often the deciding factor which prevented further progress. If there wasn't enough visibility to see the leading marks or buoys you didn't set out, or if already at sea you 'hove to' well offshore rather than closing a coast with numerous unmarked offlying dangers. For a yacht fitted with GPS the decision to put to sea in bad visibility is generally decided by whether or not you are confident that you can see enough to avoid collisions. For a boat already at sea, it should be possible to find the harbour entrance however thick the fog.

If you are caught out in really bad visibility, particularly near shipping lanes, it is sensible to modify your plans so that, as far as possible, you stay in shallow water, where large ships cannot possibly run you down. In the vicinity of a commercial port of any size it is worth listening to the VHF port operations channel: you will hear ships requesting permission to leave their berth or enter harbour and you can build up a useful picture of the traffic movements.

How narrow a channel can you safely attempt using GPS without any help from visual clues? That depends on how skilful you are at using it. Try navigating from the chart table without looking out in good visibility and ask those on deck not to tell you about navigational marks until they are within, say, 50 yards. (But do remind them to keep a good lookout for approaching ships and take positive action to avoid them.) The satellites will give you enough information to find your way and you will soon find out how good you are at using it. Not many good things in life come for free, but the GPS system is certainly one of them. Enjoy it!

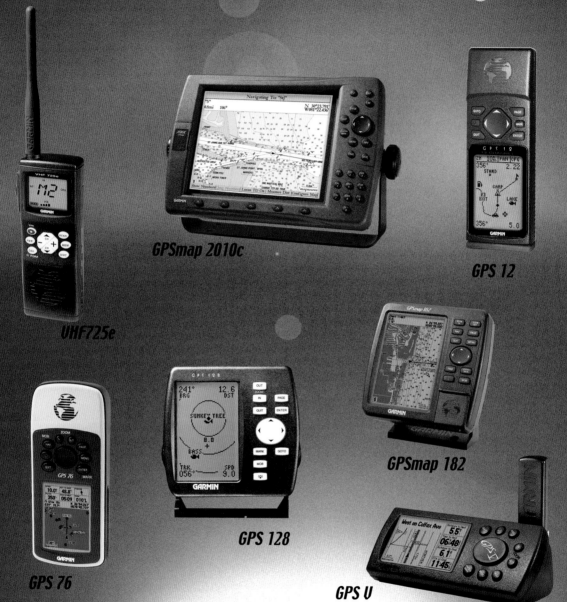

Photo: © Yachting World

"As sailors, we can always count on volunteer lifeboat crews. Can they count on you? Please join *Offshore* today."

Sir Robin Knox-Johnston CBE, RD*

However experienced you are at sea, you never know when you'll need the help of a lifeboat crew. But to keep saving lives, the Royal National Lifeboat Institution's volunteer crews need *your* help.

That is why you should join **Offshore**. For just £3.50 per month, you can help save thousands of lives, receive practical information to help keep *you* safe at sea *and* save money on equipment for your boat. *Please join us today.*

Please join *Offshore* – today

Please photocopy and return this form, with your payment if appropriate, to: RNLI, FREEPOST, West Quay Road, Poole, Dorset BH15 1XF.

Mr/Mrs/Miss/Ms [   ] Initial [   ] Surname [   ]

Address [   ]

[   ] Postcode [   ]

I would like to join:

☐ As an *Offshore* member at £ [   ] per month/quarter/year * (min £4.00 per month/£12 per quarter/£48 per year)

☐ As Joint *Offshore* members at £ [   ] per month/quarter/year *

(Husband & Wife, min £7 per month/£21 per quarter/£84 per year) * please delete as applicable

Please debit the above sum as indicated from my Visa/MasterCard * now and at the prevailing rate until cancelled by me in writing.

Card No. [   ] Expiry date [/   ]

Signature [   ]

(Please give address of cardholder on a separate piece of paper if different from above.)

Alternatively, I wish to pay my **Offshore** membership by cheque/PO

I enclose a cheque/Postal Order for £ [   ] payable to Royal National Lifeboat Institution.

Or, I wish to pay my subscription by Direct Debit ☐

Please tick the box – a Direct Debit form will be sent to you.   FERN11

Lifeboats
Offshore

Because life's not all plain sailing

Registered Charity No. 209603